# UNMASKING THE NEW AGE

## DOUGLAS R. GROOTHUIS

INTERVARSITY PRESS
DOWNERS GROVE, ILLINOIS 60515

*To Becky*

*InterVarsity Press is the book-publishing division of Inter-Varsity Christian Fellowship, a student movement active on campus at hundreds of universities, colleges and schools of nursing. For information about local and regional activities, write IVCF, 233 Langdon St., Madison, WI 53703.*

*Distributed in Canada through InterVarsity Press, 860 Denison St., Unit 3, Markham, Ontario L3R 4H1, Canada.*

*Cover illustration: Roberta Polfus*

*ISBN 0-87784-568-9*

*Printed in the United States of America*

**Library of Congress Cataloguing in Publication Data**
Groothuis, Douglas, 1957–
  Unmasking the new age.

  Bibliography: p.
  Includes index.
  1. Cults.  2. Monism.  I. Title.
BP603.G76     1986          291          85-23832
ISBN 0-87784-568-9

17   16   15   14   13   12   11   10   9   8   7
99   98   97   96   95   94   93   92   91   90   89   88   87

# Foreword

Advertising that it can transform people and society worldwide, the New Age movement is spearheading a comprehensive attack on many of the highest values of both the Christian church and Western culture. For about two decades Eastern religions have been moving West and aggressively seeking converts among secularists and Christians. Now a kind of ecumenical movement of Eastern, occult and New Consciousness groups network together in the New Age movement.

"New" primarily to secular humanists in the West, the basic New Age assumption is older than history. Its belief that "all is one" has many serious implications. It challenges the reality of our distinct personhood, the world we observe and the distinction between good and evil. According to the New Age scheme, what we can understand and express conceptually—about the family, nature, history and the Bible itself—becomes the enemy of mystical experience. To experience "oneness" we must do away not only with our uniqueness as persons but also with our capacity for conceptual and critical thinking.

In *Unmasking the New Age* Douglas Groothuis has clearly revealed the terminal disease at the heart of the New Age movement (monism) and helpfully diagnosed the symptoms in its extremities: holistic health, transpersonal psychology, deified energy in physics, a politically unified world order and a spirituality that is really narcissistic self-worship. In this perceptive and well-researched book Groothuis helps Christians become more alert and discerning without becoming alarmist.

I believe God will use *Unmasking the New Age* to deliver many pre-Christians from the futile quest for spirituality without the guidance of the biblical gospel. It will also deliver many from the illusion of universal and permanent peace independent of the transcendent, personal Lord of all.

As Emile Cailliet, a former French atheist, found, "Either a life is in line with the Word of God or one's spirituality is likely to dwindle to little more than a confusing panpsychic experience, that of the dynamism of nature reflected in one's soul." (*Journey into Light* [Grand Rapids, Mich.: Zondervan, 1968], p. 30.)

Perhaps an even greater service *Unmasking the New Age* will provide is preventive. I realized the great importance of prevention as a visiting professor in India where the results of a monistic world view and way of life have been entrenched for centuries. In a rural area of that poverty-stricken culture human life was cheap. I could see how difficult it is to evangelize pantheists who believe that they are already divine, have endless potential for self-improvement, are not inherently sinful, and not in need of the gracious, once-for-all provision of Jesus Christ's atonement. I began to understand why after two hundred years of missionary work, only some four per cent of the world's second largest population is in any sense of the word Christian. This volume shows how important it is to keep monism from becoming dominant in schools, homes, businesses, governments and churches. Its ounce of prevention in time can be worth a ton of corrective cures!

*Unmasking the New Age* challenges Christian leaders to develop and teach a sound theistic world and life view. Christians will not adequately counter the New Age world view and way of life with slogans and bumper stickers. This book should move young people and adults in churches and schools to put the bits and pieces of

Christian truth together in a comprehensive Christian belief system. This system should incorporate revealed truth relevant to physical and psychological health, physics, politics and spirituality.

This carefully written book also challenges Christians to develop a method of preevangelism like that of Paul among the Stoic pantheists in first-century Athens. We cannot assume that New Age people understand what we mean when we say, "For *God* so loved the world." Like Paul at Athens we must first help New Age people understand that they are dependent on a transcendent, personal Creator, accountable to him and guilty before him. Only then can we intelligibly call them to repent for their sins, believe the gospel, and trust Jesus Christ whom God has raised from the dead (Acts 17:16-31).

God forbid that in this "new age" of unparalleled opportunity and challenge evangelicals will do too little too late!

Gordon R. Lewis
professor of theology and philosophy
and founder of Evangelical Ministries to New Religions, Inc.
Denver Seminary
Denver, Colorado
November 1985

# Acknowledgments

Many deserve thanks for their assistance in this work. Howard Ahmanson helped finance the writing of the book. Other supporters include Mike Scully, Leona Boyd, Linda Leonard, Gordon and Sandra Mallon, and my grandparents, Ann Groothuis and John Cominetto. The McKenzie Study Center in Eugene, Oregon, served as a research and support base for me in much of my work. I particularly thank staff members Greg Spencer and Wes Hurd for their friendship and advice. A fellow worker in campus ministry, Richard Beswick, was always a source of encouragement and a pleasure to work with.

Thanks go to IVP editor James W. Sire for encouragement and advice given to an insecure new author. I also thank Michael Maudlin for his excellent editorial midwifery.

I owe the Spiritual Counterfeits Project of Berkeley, California, a great debt of gratitude for educating me on the variety of New Age spiritual counterfeits. Their pioneering work was inspiring.

I wish to thank my mother, Lillian Groothuis, for the countless ways she shows her love. Jean and Paul Merrill have been mighty prayer warriors and have shown special love and encouragement.

It was my wife, Becky, who—before we were even married—prodded me to finally start writing and volunteered to edit the chapters as I went along. Her editorial, emotional and spiritual contributions have been invaluable. It could not have been done without her.

# The One
# for All

**1**

P ICTURE TWENTY-FIVE NORMAL FIRST-GRADERS PEACEFULLY LYING IN SILENCE on their classroom floor. It's not a fire drill or an air raid, but part of the new curriculum. The children are being guided through a meditation in which they are instructed to imagine the sun radiantly shining toward them. They are then told to gaze into its brightness without being hurt by the light. Next the children are asked to try to bring the sun down into their bodies and feel its warmth, power, illumination.

"Imagine that you are doing something perfect," the teacher commands, "and that you are perfect."

The children are told to see themselves as resplendent with light; they should feel at peace, for they are perfect. They "are reminded that they are intelligent, magnificent, and that they contain all of the wisdom of the universe within themselves."[1]

This "exercise" actually took place in a Los Angeles public school. The designer of the meditation, the late Beverly Galyean, desired to apply her federally funded "confluent education" to the masses of students who need an "expanded view of learning."² This isn't prayer, since prayer is forbidden; but neither is it the three R's. What is behind Galyean's approach? She tells us herself:

> Once we begin to see that we are all God, that we all have the attributes of God, then I think the whole purpose of human life is to reown the Godlikeness within us; the perfect love, the perfect wisdom, the perfect understanding, the perfect intelligence, and when we do that, we create back to that old, that essential oneness which is consciousness.³

## On the March

Galyean's "confluent education" isn't an isolated case. Nor can she be written off as merely strange or weird. Rather, this is just one of the many manifestations of a fast growing, insurgent world view that promises to engulf the globe. Not only are schoolchildren affected, but so is all of society. A philosophically united confederacy has begun to converge on Western culture and promises to radically transform both the consciousness and character of the modern world. Examples of this world-view shift, frequently described as "the New Age movement," are not far from our everyday experience.

We all know Shirley MacLaine. She danced in the movie *The Turning Point;* she swooned in *Being There;* she played the quirky mother in *Terms of Endearment;* she was part of a government-selected delegation to China; she's won several Emmy Awards; and she's written two books that chronicle her conversion to a "New Age" view of things, *Out on a Limb* and *Dancing in the Light.* A reluctant convert, MacLaine was coaxed into a belief in reincarnation and basic occult philosophy through a series of extraordinary events: out-of-the-body experiences; trance-channeling (séances) with various spirits who discoursed on the nature of God, man and the world; friendships with many New Age sojourners; and reading a host of books on the occult, mysticism, reincarnation and much else.

Her "search for identity" has led her to affirm that "nothing is more powerful than the collective human mind."[4] Her central message is fourfold: first, you are gods (although you might be ignorant of it); second, you have lived before and will live again; third, there is no death ("Perhaps our belief in death is the greatest unreality of all"[5]); fourth, there are as many realities as there are people since we create our own reality. To promote *Out on a Limb,* MacLaine became omnipresent in the media—visiting television and radio talk shows, giving magazine interviews and appearing as the subject of many articles. She has become a celebrity evangelist for the New Age.

We can see an undercurrent of expectation and excitement throughout the academic disciplines and among people in general. There is a growing consensus that the modern world is on the brink of the extraordinary and that a great transformation awaits us. Check the magazine rack of a local health-food store or visit an occult bookstore and you'll find this unifying thread of belief. Browse through current magazines—*New Age, Yoga Journal, East-West Journal, New Realities, Whole Life Times* or even *Science Digest*—and you'll find it. Consider the number of articles about ESP, altered states of consciousness, the new physics and Eastern religions that are appearing in establishment magazines. Ask a friend who meditates or follows astrology, or even many prominent physicists, what it's all about and you'll get basically the same answer. Peruse the psychology, philosophy and science sections of any major bookstore and notice how they have many of the same titles that are in the Eastern religion and occult sections.

Whether from Eastern religions, the occult, the new psychologies, the "frontier" theories of science, New Age politics or New Age versions of Christianity, various ideas with a common theme are converging on our culture, pressing their way to the philosophical and ideological center of society. A new world view is in the offing; a revolution in consciousness beckons. All is one—both good and evil. We are all god—and our first-graders should know it. The mind controls all—if we only use it. These are ideas—potent ideas—that have consequences for the whole of life. They are shaping the lives of more and more Westerners.

This reality, this "New Consciousness," is hoping to bring about a "New Age" of hope and human fulfillment. New Age advocates argue that the West has been locked in a prison of the ordinary and one-dimensional, separated from the mystical vitality of a universe of harmonious dancing energy. The problems besetting the modern world—the threat of nuclear holocaust, world hunger, ecological devastation, psychological breakdowns—are blamed on a false and rapidly decaying world view, an outmoded perspective on life. Those sleeping must be awakened before the sleep turns to death. The old ways and views are impotent. They cannot rescue modern humanity.

**Mapping Our World**
Before outlining the world view of this New Consciousness, we need to understand the effect of any world view on culture. Psychologist Erich Fromm remarks that a society's "social character must fulfill any human being's inherent religious needs" and that all cultures have a basic and inescapable religious underpinning, whatever that religion might be.[6] Religion, according to Fromm, is *"any group shared system of thought and action that offers the individual a frame of orientation and an object of devotion.* Indeed, in this broad sense of the word no culture of the past or present, and it seems no culture of the future, can be considered as not having religion."[7]

Some religion or another will govern society. As Fromm puts it, "The question is not one of *religion or not?* but of which kind of religion?"[8] He goes on to say that the human species needs "a map of our natural and social world—a picture of the world and of one's place in it."[9] Without it we would be condemned to perpetual indecision and vertigo.

This "frame of orientation" or "religion" involves a *world view* which can be defined as "a set of presuppositions (or assumptions) which we hold (consciously or subconsciously) about the basic make-up of the world."[10] Our world view bears necessarily on everything we do, as Ayn Rand insightfully notes:

> Consciously or subconsciously, explicitly or implicitly, man knows that he needs a comprehensive view of existence to integrate his values, to choose his goals, to plan his future, to maintain the unity and coherence of his life—and that his metaphysical value-judgments are involved in every moment of his life, in his every choice, decision and action.[11]

Although many people may deny that they have any "comprehensive view of existence," they nevertheless follow one; they must. Their values are based on what they deem as true and real whether or not they have thought these things through.

Society as a whole likewise functions according to basic underlying assumptions about reality. Ironically, the power and importance of a society's world view may be unnoticed and therefore uninspected. As Jeremy Rifkin notes, "The most interesting aspect of society's world view is that its individual adherents are, for the most part, unconscious of how it affects the way they do things and how they perceive the reality around them."[12]

Yet if this New Consciousness claims to provide the desperately needed world view to bring about the New Age, we must diligently see what it affirms and why, lest we credulously follow its dictates without giving it a thought.

Everywhere the New Age tells us that we face a "transformation." Our conceptual, political and economic structures must be rethought and re-experienced. As Lewis Mumford has said: "Every transformation of man, except perhaps that which produced the neolithic culture, has rested on a new metaphysical and ideological base; or rather, upon deeper stirrings and intuitions whose rationalised expression takes the form of a new picture of the cosmos and the nature of man."[13] What is the "new picture of the cosmos and man" put forth by New Age adherents?

The task of properly identifying, analyzing and critiquing something as large and varied as the New Age movement is a formidable task for several reasons. First, the New Age movement is quite eclectic; it draws from many sources. While unifying themes can be uncovered, there is also great diversity. Second, because of this diversity, statements made by representatives of the New Age may not hold for all those associated with it. Third, the New Age world view itself emphasizes and exalts change and evolution. Therefore, many of those involved in the New Age movement often shift their perspectives, making their ideas sometimes hard to pin down. Nevertheless, we can identify six distinctives of New Age thinking. I will present each point and contrast it from a Christian world view. Then in the next chapter we will view the history of this movement, and in the following chapters we will explore the specific ways this world view is trying to enter our society: through the health industry, psychology, science, politics and the new spirituality. Finally in the last chapter we will see how we as Christians can challenge the New Age movement.

## 1. All Is One

The idea that "all is one" is foundational for the New Age; it permeates the movement in all its various manifestations—from holistic health to the new physics, from politics to transpersonal psychology, from Eastern religions to the occult. Another name for this idea is *monism. Mono* means "one." Monism, then, is the belief that all that is, is one. All is interrelated, interdependent and interpenetrating. Ultimately there is no difference between God, a person, a carrot or a rock. They are all part of one continuous reality that has no boundaries, no ultimate divisions. Any perceived differences between separate entities—between Joe and Judy or between Joe and a tree or between God and Judy—are only apparent and not real.

We can find this idea graphically expressed in, of all places, the children's movie *The Dark Crystal* (produced by Jim Henson, the creator of the Muppets). It is essentially a fairy tale of monism. In it we find two groups of creatures, the Mystics and the Skecsees, who represent the two rival ruling factions in the land. The Mystics, lovable and slow-moving contemplatives, spend their time chanting and giving sagacious advice. The Skecsees are evil and depraved: wretched gluttons and power-craving monsters.

Yet all is not so simple. As the story unfolds we see that a gimling has found the lost chard once split off from the planet's magic crystal. After many perilous adventures he returns the lost chard to the crystal. With the unity of the crystal restored, we witness a major transformation. The Mystics and the Skecsees are fused into one unified group of beings. Good and evil are transcended and cosmic unity is restored. We are told in no uncertain terms that good does not overcome evil, as in so many fairy tales; good and evil are really one and the same. The Skecsees, for all their apparent depravity, were not evil but only the dark side of the Mystics. Likewise, the Mystics were not good in themselves; they had to be reunited with the Skecsees. All is one; ultimate reality is beyond good and evil. This is the essential teaching of much of Eastern religion and occultism, and it is being advocated by a host of New Age scientists. The physicist and philosopher Fritjof Capra says in his book *The Turning Point* that the ultimate state of consciousness is one "in which all boundaries and dualisms have been transcended and all individuality dissolves into universal, undifferentiated oneness."[14] There are not many selves but one Self, the One.

Monism, the basic premise of the New Age movement, is radically at odds with a Christian view of reality. A Christian world view affirms that God's creation is not an undivided unity but rather a created diversity of objects, events and persons. Genesis 1 records God creating particular things. God separated the light from the darkness, day from night, the earth from the sky and the dry ground from the seas.

He then created plants and animals according to their various kinds. Finally, he created humans in his image. Creation is thus not a homogeneous soup of undifferentiated unity but a created *plurality*. Creation is not unified in itself but in the plan and purpose of God—in Christ "all things hold together" (Col 1:17). Our world is, as C. S. Lewis put it, "incorrigibly plural."15 Even God himself, according to the Bible, is not an undifferentiated unity but a tri-unity of Father, Son and Holy Spirit—the Trinity.

## 2. All Is God

Once we admit that all is one, including god, then it is a short step to admitting that "all is god." This is pantheism. All things—plants, snails, books and so on—are said to partake of the one divine essence. Remember our schoolchildren who were told to imagine themselves as perfect beings. How could it be otherwise? All is one; all is god. Whatever is, is god and therefore perfect.

Going further, it is argued that if everything is one and if all dualities in reality dissolve into the cosmic unity, then so does the idea of personality. A personality can only exist where it defines itself in relation to other beings or things. Even self-consciousness demands some form of a relationship. But if all is one, then there is only one being—the One. The One does not have a personality; it is beyond personality. God is more an "it" than a "he." The idea of a personal God is abandoned in favor of an impersonal energy, force or consciousness. Ultimate reality is god, who is in all and through all; in fact, god is all.

Yet the Bible affirms that all is not god. God the Creator stands transcendently distinct from his creation. While God is present in his creation—not being an absentee landlord—he is not to be confused with the creation. Creation does not contain him. The apostle Paul spoke against those who "exchanged the truth of God for a lie, and worshiped and served created things rather than the Creator" (Rom 1:25). The book of Ecclesiastes tells us that "God is in heaven and you are on earth" (5:2). To identify what is not God as God is what the Bible calls "idolatry."

C. S. Lewis put it well: "Pantheism is a creed not so much false as hopelessly behind the times. Once, before creation, it would have been true to say that everything was God. But God created: He caused things to be other than Himself."[16] Creation is derived from its Creator, depending on him for both its origin and continued existence; it has no independent existence.

The Creator God is not an impersonal force, energy or consciousness, but a living, personal Being of infinite intelligence, power and purity. God is not an amoral entity, but a moral agent who says "Thou shalt not" and calls people to repentance and faith.

## 3. Humanity Is God

This is one of the seductive claims of the New Age: we are not only perfect; we are, in fact, gods. Philosopher and New Age precursor L. L. Whyte is forthright: "It has long been held that whoever denies [the transcendent] God asserts his own divinity. In dropping God, man recovers himself. It is time that God be put in his place, that is, *in man*, and no nonsense about it."[17] Author Paul Williams provides this cosmic quip: "Remember, but not for the grace of God, we would not be God. It's something to think about."[18]

We are god in disguise. Only ignorance keeps us from realizing our divine reality. Our goal, according to New Age analyst Theodore Roszak, is "to awaken to the god who sleeps at the root of the human being."[19] Swami Muktananda—a great influence on Werner Erhard, founder of est and Forum—pulls no pantheistic punches when he says: "Kneel to your own self. Honor and worship your own being. God dwells within you as You!"[20]

Whether it comes from Eastern religions such as Hinduism—"Atman is Brahman" (the individual self is really the universal Self)—or from classical occultism—"as above, so below" (God and humanity are one)—or from the new self-actualizing psychologies—all knowledge, power and truth are within and waiting to be unlocked—the New Age raises the placard of pantheism high: you are god! Stewart Brand, writing in the introduction to the popular *The Next Whole Earth Catalogue,* says, "We are as Gods and might as well get good at it."[21] This is the "good news" the New Age has to preach. According to George Leonard, long-time New Age activist and author, each of us "is the entire universe," and "we are like a God, omnipotent and omniscient."[22]

But the truth is that humanity is not God. Christianity affirms that though human beings are made in the image of God (Gen 1:26), they are not in essence God. We reflect our Creator in that we, like him, are personal—we think, feel and act. But we are not infinite, all-powerful, all-knowing or everywhere present. We are finite and personal, whereas God is infinite and personal. We are creatures; he is the Creator. Divinity must not be confused with humanity. The Bible repeatedly condemns human pretenders to the divine throne (Is 14:13-15; Ezek 28:1-2; Acts 12:21-23).

## 4. A Change in Consciousness

All is one; all is god; we are god. Simple enough? Then why don't we know ourselves as gods? What is our problem? The answer is simple: ignorance. Western culture has shaped our consciousness, trimming our experience and taming our metaphysics. We remain content with the everyday illusions of human limitation and finitude. We need to be enlightened. We have forgotten our true identity.

But there is hope. This metaphysical amnesia can be reversed by techniques designed to alter ordinary consciousness. These techniques open "the doors of perception" so that we can see true reality. This change in consciousness, whatever the means, leads to an awareness of oneness and spiritual power.

There are many ways we can achieve this enlightenment. Even sports, the all-American pastimes of brawn and skill, have become a theater for this kind of change in consciousness. Michael Murphy, founder of the Esalen Institute in northern California, has studied the experiences of athletes and concludes that extreme physical achievement, whether it be in baseball, football, golf, skiing or whatever, can induce a mystical state of consciousness much like that spoken of in Eastern religions. He says in his book *The Psychic Side of Sports* that "the many reports we have collected show us that sport has enormous power to sweep us beyond the ordinary sense of self, to evoke capacities that have generally been regarded as mystical, occult, or religious."[23]

Murphy speaks of "the spiritual underground of sports" wherein altered states of consciousness or even supernatural feats occur. He notes that John Brodie, former star quarterback for the San Francisco Forty-niners, experienced profound changes in consciousness during games. Murphy compares these extraordinary experiences with those of Eastern yoga and finds a great similarity.[24] He says, "The East now meets the West on very ordinary ground: right here in the human body." Later he adds that "most of the vivid new religious thrusts have to do with body mysticism, not with more abstract forms of belief that were once the grist of revivalism. God is not dead, He is in the gut."[25] Murphy is almost messianic about the potential that sports unleashes; he believes that it may be "the beginning of a human unfoldment that will eventually extend its boundaries in all areas of life."[26]

But this change in consciousness is not limited to the playing field. It can also take place in a scientist's laboratory. Fritjof Capra, after having an experience that altered his understanding of the universe, describes how what had previously been scientific theories became for him a mystical reality: "I 'saw' the atoms of the elements and those of my body participating in this cosmic dance of energy; I felt its rhythm and I 'heard' its sound, and at that moment *I knew* that this was the dance of Shiva, the Lord of Dancers worshipped by the Hindus."[27] For Capra the *experience* of oneness ("the Dance of Shiva") compelled him to attempt a reconciliation and marriage between modern high-energy physics and Eastern mysticism.

Even UFO or supposed extraterrestrial contact may result in a conversion to New Age philosophy. Shirley MacLaine, for instance, claims that her book *Out on a Limb* was indirectly inspired by an extraterrestrial named "the Mayan."

To gain this type of transformation, the three ideas that all is one, all is god, and we are god must be more than intellectual propositions; they must be awakened at the core of our being. Such an experience may be either spontaneous and unplanned or the result of disciplined practice in meditation, yoga or some other consciousness-raising technique.

Mass training sessions such as est (Erhard Seminars Training) have been a popular method of triggering this change of awareness. (It should be noted that Werner Erhard has announced that he has replaced est with a new program called Forum.) In the est experience several hundred people are brought together for two successive weekends of marathon sessions designed to help them get "it." During the sessions they are confined to their chairs for long hours without note-taking, talking, smoking, clock-watching or sitting next to anyone they know. Minimal food and bathroom breaks are strictly observed.

Each of the sixteen-hour sessions is led by a trainer who berates, taunts and humiliates the crowd by insisting that their lives don't work. The sustained intensity leads many to become sick, cry or break down in some other way. That's the goal. Through the agonizing hours of torture the tears turn to insight and the sickness into enlightenment. The participants are told, "You're part of every atom in the world and every atom is part of you. We are all gods who created our own worlds."[28] Eventually the people—at least some of them—claim to get "it"; they experience enlightenment and oneness. From 1971 to 1981, 325,000 people from the United States, Europe, the Middle East and Asia were "ested," including celebrities such as Yoko Ono, Carly Simon, Diana Ross and John Denver, who is a self-appointed evangelist for the cause.[29]

But est is only one of numerous means of experiencing a revolution in consciousness. Scores of people are chanting, dancing or tripping their way into altered states of awareness. They may use self-hypnotism, internal visualization, biofeedback or even the sexual act.[30] There are many names for this transforming experience: cosmic consciousness, God-realization, self-realization, enlightenment, illumination, Nirvana (Buddhist), satori (Zen), at-one-ment or satchitananada (Hindu).

But whatever the name, this new level of awareness is said to be vital for the resurrection of Western civilization and the world. The old consciousness of Western rationalism has stripped the world of mystic meaning. Only through a resurrection of consciousness will the world be raised out of the modern miry pit. As the popular New Age radio program "New Dimensions" says in their introduction, "It is only through a change of consciousness that the world will be changed. This is our responsibility."

And what are we to do? We are to look within. As one New Age ad put it, "The only way out is in." All is perfect, says Werner Erhard. The trouble is we don't *see it.* Humans are not depraved or dependent on any outside source of deliverance or strength. The answer is not reconciliation with a God different from ourselves, but the realization that we ourselves are God. The self is the cosmic treasury of wisdom, power and delight.

This realization of oneness and divinity leads to spiritual power and well-being. Tension subsides, claims transcendental meditation, when one meditates twice daily. The true god-self consumes the troubles of everyday life. But often the claims of the New Age embrace far more than natural well-being. In 1977 transcendental meditation offered a Sidhi program which promised advanced students the ability to levitate, fly and become invisible.

Such claims are not unique. Once the true knowledge (or *gnosis*) of reality is realized, higher powers are activated within. The limitations of a supposedly finite and imperfect being fade into the limitless potential of the truly enlightened being. The awesome expanses of parapsychology open before us: telepathy, ESP, precognition, telekinesis and others. Alan Vaughan, writing in *Futurist* magazine, claims that once precognition (predicting the future) "has emerged from the world of the strange into the everyday world of business, government, education, and science, the stage will be set for a new leap forward: An enlightened society will have the wisdom to foresee and fulfill its best future."[31]

Shirley MacLaine captures this spirit: "We already know everything. The knowingness of our divinity is the highest intelligence. And to *be* what we already know is the free will. Free will is simply the enactment of the realization you are God, a realization that you are divine: free will is making everything accessible to you."[32] Everything and anything is potentially accessible. We all create our own reality. To use an older phrase, it is mind over matter.

If this change of consciousness depends on our grasping and experiencing some truth, we must ask ourselves what role does our mind play or our reason? Some teachings of the New Age seem contradictory: that there are many realities and that all is one. Some reply that ordinary logic doesn't apply to the higher states of consciousness; in fact, it may hinder the raising of consciousness. The influential guru Bhagwan Shree Rajneesh puts it strongly: "It is not that the intellect sometimes misunderstands. Rather, the intellect always misunderstands. It is not that the intellect sometimes errs; it is that the intellect is the error. It always errs."[33] Though some may qualify this statement, New Age thinkers agree that the One is beyond what the normal intellect can grasp. It must be experienced, not discussed.

Christianity also affirms that we need a change in consciousness, though it differs in seeing what this entails. Biblically, the dilemma of humanity is not ignorance of our true divinity, but the reality of our sin; we have rebelled against a holy God and his moral law. The problem, not the answer, is within. Jesus said that out of our hearts proceeds all evil (Mk 7:22–23). The Fall of humanity recorded in Genesis 3 gives the pattern of human rebellion against the legitimate authority of God—independence is declared from God and his law in favor of self-law. Since then, as Paul says, "all have sinned and fall short of the glory of God" (Rom 3:23).

The New Age sees the answer to this dilemma in releasing human potential—the divine within. But Christianity claims that the only way out is through repentance and faith in Jesus Christ—God made flesh. Salvation is the process by which we gain a new consciousness, and it is found in Christ—"Behold, I make all things new" (Rev 21:5 RSV). Though sinless, Christ bore the sins of the world on the cross to make way for sinful humanity to be reconciled to a holy God. Christ offered himself in love for those who cannot please God by their own sinful works (2 Cor 5:21). Jesus taught that whoever believes in him could know the forgiveness of sins and have eternal life, the life he himself foreshadowed by his own resurrection (Jn 3:16).

Jesus did not teach "at-one-ment" with the One (losing individuality), but atonement with God through his sacrificial death on the cross. Neither does one need to dissolve logical thought to approach God. God, as a personal and rational being, reveals himself in understandable propositions in the Bible. But one must approach God with humility if anything is to be discovered, for "God opposes the proud but gives grace to the humble" (Jas 4:6).

The Bible warns us about approaching the spiritual dimension apart from Christ (see Acts 19:13–16). The New Age's appeal to psychic power opens a Pandora's box of paranormal poisons which the Bible prohibits (Lev 19:26, 31; Deut 18:10–12). The demonic spiritual realm opens wide before the unprotected psychic sojourner with numerous counterfeit charms declared "off-limits" by a loving Creator.

## 5. All Religions Are One

New Age gurus frequently claim that all religions are one and, at their core, teach the One for all. This is called syncretism. Certainly if all is one, all is god, and we are god, we should expect that the enlightened ones of all the great religions—Jesus, Buddha, Lao-tse, Krishna and others—would have taught and experienced the same oneness. The externals of religions may differ, but the essence is the same. There may be many paths to the one truth, many methods to become one with the One, but all differences are superficial and external. Dogmas may come and go, but the vital experience of "the god within" is common throughout the world. This "perennial philosophy," as Aldous Huxley called it, is said to undergird the experiences throughout history of Hindus, Buddhists, Hebrews, Taoists, Christians and Muslims.

Consequently, the distinctiveness of Christianity must be denied. Claims of uniqueness and exclusiveness must be dissolved into the cosmic unity. Philosopher Jacob Needleman and guru Da Free John speak of a "lost Christianity," which turns out to be little different from Eastern mysticism and occultism. This, they proclaim, is the true but suppressed reality of Jesus. A recent book by Elaine Pagels, _The Gnostic Gospels_, champions Gnosticism, an early Christian heresy, as the true form of faith and experience. The Jesus of the Gnostics was little different from a Hindu sage. The Gospel of Thomas reports Jesus saying: "It is I who am the light which is above them all. It is I who am the All. From Me did the All come forth, and unto Me did the All extend. Split a piece of wood, and I am there. Lift up the stone, and you will find Me there."[34]

Jesus of Nazareth, then, is no longer said to be the only begotten Son of God, the God-man, the Lord and Savior of the cosmos. He is merely one of many appearances or manifestations of God throughout the millennia. His mission was to alert the sleeping masses to their innate divinity. Jesus is thus reverentially enshrined in the pantheistic pantheon where he echoes the chorus of the enlightened: all is one. The Christ of the Bible is redefined and made the ventriloquist's puppet for the New Age. Christ as the mediator between God and humanity is replaced with the idea of "Christ-consciousness," which is another word for cosmic consciousness. Likewise, the biblical teaching of eternal judgment (heaven or hell) is replaced by reincarnation in much New Age thought.

But the Christ of the Bible is not merely one of many manifestations of God. In fact, Christ is the *only* manifestation of God in the flesh. He claimed to be "the way and the truth and the life" and that no one could know God's favor apart from him (Jn 14:6). The apostle Peter declared that "salvation is found in no one else, for there is no other name under heaven given to men by which we must be saved" (Acts 4:12). Christ will not join the pantheistic pantheon, but instead stands above it in judgment. His exclusivity is our liberation because he calls all to himself.

## 6. Cosmic Evolutionary Optimism

Over twenty-five years ago, Julian Huxley, avowed secular humanist and defender of rational science as the interpreter of all of life, laid the motivational groundwork for the New Age. He said, "Man is that part of reality in which and through which the cosmic process has become conscious and has begun to comprehend itself. His supreme task is to increase that conscious comprehension and to apply it as fully as possible to guide the course of events."[35]

Huxley was far from a mystic in the New Age sense; yet his vision has sparked the New Age movement with optimism and hope. As this philosophy gains ground and infiltrates all of life with the gospel of cosmic unity, it is predicted that humanity will be ready to take over the reins of evolution. Teilhard de Chardin, Jesuit philosopher and paleontologist, prophesied a progressive evolutionary harmonization and unification of world consciousness eventually reaching "the Omega Point" where all consciousness is fused and all become one with the One.

Teilhard, a patron saint of the New Age—though deemed unorthodox and suppressed by the Roman Catholic Church—is just one of many seers, sages, scientists and others who predict massive trans-formation. The evolutionary juices are flowing. William Irwin Thompson is expectant: "Whether the movement from one world-system to another will involve stumbling or total collapse may very well depend on the success or failure of the new age movement. Now as we stand poised at the edge ∩f a great transformation, we are prophetically inspired and politically armoured as never before."[36] The time is right for change. George Leonard sees the potential: "The current period is indeed unique in history and . . . represents the beginning of the most thoroughgoing change in the quality of human existence since the creation of an agricultural surplus brought about the birth of civilized states some five thousand years ago."[37]

A variety of futurists, notably Barbara Marx Hubbard and Willis Harman, expect a New Age to dawn, rising out of the ashes of the old Western world view. Hubbard warns that global problems are increasing exponentially; yet, at the same time, our potentials are also growing exponentially. We must move beyond the "crisis futurism" of doomsday scenarios in which we are seen as "poor lost riders mounted upon a wild horse of transformation with little hope of gaining control."[38] Instead we must embrace a "spiritual futurism" which incorporates all the strength of "evolutionary futurism" (hope for radical evolutionary change). With millions now "actively praying, listening to inner intuition, expanding their awareness toward whole-centered consciousness," we see that evolution itself is "a conscious-ness-raising experience."[39] We may even expect a new suprahuman species which will be "as superior to present day humanity as we are to the apes."[40]

As consciousness changes, so will the future. In her book *The Evo-lutionary Journey* Hubbard explains what she means by "spiritual futurism": "At this moment of our planetary birth each person is called upon to recognize that the 'Messiah is within.' Christ con-sciousness or cosmic consciousness is awakening in millions of Chris-tians and non-Christians."[41] The "messiah within" will lead all of us forward into a glorious future. We should remember that Hubbard's article on "spiritual futurism" did not appear in an obscure occult newsletter, but in a mainline magazine, *The Futurist.* Even "the establishment" is becoming primed for transformation.

Christians can be both more optimistic and more pessimistic about the future than is the New Age. The Bible views history as moving according to the sovereign will of the Creator and Governor of the universe "who works out everything in conformity with the purpose of his will" (Eph 1:11). Hope for the future does not lie in realizing the potential of collective humanity but in the promises of God. God promises to bless nations that obey him and curse nations that disobey him (Deut 8, 28; Jer 18:5-10). The culmination of history will not be a great planetary consciousness but the return of Jesus Christ to separate the sheep from the goats for all eternity. For some the future will be much better than we could ever imagine—for others, much worse.

## New Age Connections
A key element of hope in the New Age agenda is the information revolution. As we move from the Industrial Age to the Information Age, the New Age hopes to cover the globe with a myriad of "networks," interconnecting ideas, people, services and organizations in order to implement world transformation.

The computer chip is hailed by many as a vital evolutionary impetus. Mass media and modern communications serve to "globalize" and unify consciousness. Technological innovation accelerates the rate of evolution and provides a needed context for the New Consciousness. William Irwin Thompson believes that the "electronic envelope" that now surrounds and permeates the earth is the fulfillment of Teilhard de Chardin's prophecy of the development of the "noosphere" (the expanding layer of consciousness on earth). Thompson says that the informational structures now in place reflect an inward change: "The mystic and the artist know that human consciousness is not standing still, and that in many ways our informational technologies are simply gross externalizations of more subtle and esoteric transformations of culture and consciousness."[42]

Marilyn Ferguson, an exuberant instigator and reporter for the New Age, finds these networks and "networking" to be crucial for transformation. As the New Age is aligned in new ways, new patterns of organization emerge, connected by "little clusters and loose networks." Yet this is not to be underestimated; she claims there are "tens of thousands of entry points" serving to band together the like-minded.[43] Networking is done by "conferences, phone calls, air travel, books, phantom organizations, papers, pamphleteering, photocopying, lectures, workshops, parties, grapevines, mutual friends, summit meetings, coalitions, tapes, newsletters."[44]

These interconnections help to spread the "transformative vision," as those sharing concerns about health, politics, ecology, psychology or any number of other subjects join together to be "antidotes to alienation" and "generate power enough to remake society."[45]

Ferguson refers to the present webs as SPINS (Segmented Polycentric Integrated Networks).[46] Neither bureaucracy nor hierarchy, these networks have the power of a lion and the cunning of a fox.

> Just as a bureaucracy is less than the sum of its parts, a network is many times greater than the sum of its parts. This is a source of power never before tapped in history: multiple self-sufficient social movements linked for a whole array of goals whose accomplishment would transform every aspect of contemporary life.[47]

Judging from the listings in books such as *The New Age Source Book* and *New Age Directory*, thousands of groups are in some sense connected with the New Age agenda. These networks, Barbara Marx Hubbard believes, will form a matrix for radical transformation. At some time, she thinks the networks will network, and the new linkages will lead to a "sudden shift" and "the apparently rapid appearance of a new order."[48]

## Is It a Conspiracy?

Networks link together a host of New Age groups and help solidify the movement. A sampling of groups identifying with New Age ideas would include most holistic health associations (American Holistic Health Medical Association, The East-West Academy of Healing Arts, the Mandala Society, the Association of Holistic Health), political action groups (World Goodwill, Planetary Citizens, Unity in Diversity Council), consciousness-raising groups (Lifespring, est, transcendental meditation, Silva Mind Control), think tanks (Esalen Institute, Naropa Institute, SRI [though it does a lot of work totally unconnected with the New Age], Lorain Association, Findhorn, Lindisfarne Association), religious groups (Eckankar, Ananda Marga Yoga Society, Scientology, Church Universal and Triumphant, and followers of the gurus Rajneesh, Da Free John, Sri Chinmoy). This doesn't include a host of grassroots organizations sprinkled throughout the country and the world. But is it a conspiracy?

Much Christian interest in the New Age has centered around various conspiracy theories. Because of the pervasiveness and influence of New Age ideas, it would not be unnatural to assume that some level of conspiracy was afoot. But we must keep in mind that conspiracy theories of all shapes, styles and sizes have been crisscrossing the planet throughout history. Any group that has transnational allegiances (such as Freemasons, Jews, Roman Catholics and international bankers) has been targeted as the elite conspirators plotting world takeover. New Age conspiracy charges simply transfer this thinking into a more modern context.

Levels of conspiracy are natural to like-minded people and groups. The New Age makes much of networking—linking ideas and people together for greater influence and creativity. This is nothing new. Christians work together to further the kingdom of God. Communists work together to expand their regime. Those linked by ideology want to implement a common agenda. But conspiratorial speculations should be tempered by several cautions.

First, every New Age group is not consciously working with all the others to take over the world. New Age individuals and groups share common goals, but they do not always have common strategies for achieving them.

Second, what conspiracy theories have in sophistication they usually lack in concrete evidence. Showing connections between people and groups is one thing; showing conspiracy is another. Richard Hofstadter commented that conspiracy thinking "is nothing if not coherent—in fact, the paranoid mentality is far more coherent than the real world, since it leaves no room for mistakes, failures, or ambiguities."[49] He goes on to say that "what distinguishes the paranoid style is not, then, the absence of verifiable facts . . . but rather the curious leap in imagination that is always made at some critical point in the recital of events."[50] This makes possible "the big leap from the undeniable to the unbelievable."[51] New Age influence in our culture is undeniable; its power as a comprehensive conspiracy is less certain. God himself warned the prophet Isaiah to "not call conspiracy everything that these people call conspiracy; do not fear what they fear, and do not dread it" (Is 8:12).

But, third, even if there exists a vast comprehensive conspiracy (which is doubtful), endless conspiratorial speculation misses the point. An understanding of the New Age's influence on our culture should lead Christians to expose the error and erect Christian alternatives rather than fill in the conspiratorial map with more and more connections. That is simply a waste of time. A doctor who spends all his time diagnosing an illness without ever treating it is pathetic. After the x-ray should come the treatment, not more x-rays.

Fourth, an exaggerated emphasis on conspiracy tends to isolate one group of people as responsible for all the world's evil. Blame is shifted from all to the few—from oneself to the evil conspirators. Sin is localized in the offending group, not in everyone. New Agers may be used as scapegoats for all societal ills. Thus we are freed from our responsibility for the world's plight and immobilized at the same time—since we are not a part of the world-controlling elite, we can do nothing.[52] Scenarios of doom replace visions of hope.

But while the Bible speaks of a general conspiracy of evil against God and his rule (Ps 2:1-3), and of Satan's influence on nonbelievers (2 Cor 4:4), it never consigns the universe or history totally to demonic power. Christ, not Satan, has been given all authority in heaven and on earth (Mt 28:18-20; Col 1:15-20); God owns the earth (Ps 24:1-2); and Christ has destroyed the works of the devil (1 Jn 3:8). Christians should, then, be aware of Satan's devices (2 Cor 2:11) but fear God alone (Prov 1:7). Eric Pement comments,

> Conspiracy theories are a dime a dozen, and none of them should cause us to put down the sickle and take up the spyglass. If we must have a conspiracy, then let us be a part of it—an invading fifth column, working toward the final overthrow of darkness. Our words and actions should therefore spring not from the paranoia of the times, but from the forthright love and boldness of God.[53]

While levels of cooperation and organization exist between various groups and individuals, the New Age movement is better viewed as a world-view shift than a unified global conspiracy. This is not to minimize its influence but to recognize it as an intellectual, spiritual and cultural force to be reckoned with in all sobriety.

This movement has no uniforms, membership cards, dues or official leaders, and yet its influence is widespread and growing. In this sense, it could be compared to existentialism, a philosophical school of thought influential during the last thirty years. Just as people like Jean Paul Sartre, Albert Camus and Martin Heidegger were spokesmen for existentialism, likewise people like Marilyn Ferguson (author), Fritjof Capra (physicist-author), Shirley MacLaine (actress-author), Theodore Roszak (historian), David Spangler (author and mystic), Ken Wilber (psychological theorist) and William Irwin Thompson (historian) along with a chorus of lesser-known voices shape New Age thought today. Not all those mentioned as being involved in the New Age movement in these pages would label their ideas "New Age," and they might not agree on all points; yet they would all resonate with the idea of releasing human potential by realizing the oneness of all things. They see themselves on the vanguard of planetary transformation, as part of a new emerging culture.

Whether you are leafing through *New Age Journal* at a local health-food store, or seeing a psychologist who prescribes Eastern meditation, or have a child being taught to meditate in public schools, or have seen the movie *The Dark Crystal*, or know someone who is dying to have you read *The Aquarian Conspiracy*, you have been touched by the New Age.

The Western world is faced with a new order, a new world view, a New Age. A grand vision of planetary transformation is sparking the hearts and minds of many. The once fashionable pessimism of modern society is being jostled by an insurgent optimism, a magnetic world view. We are excitedly told we are more than we imagined and that the world is about to take a leap into the light of expanded consciousness. As Christians we must examine this new force acting on our society or face the possibility of succumbing to a non-Christian (sometimes even anti-Christian) philosophy. But before examining the New Age's influence in the specific areas of health, psychology, science, politics and spirituality, we will scrutinize its historical roots to understand the forces that propelled it into our lives.

# From the Counterculture to the New Age

## 2

$A$T THE THOUGHT OF "HIPPIES," WHAT COMES IMMEDIATELY TO MIND? ONE might remember the smell of incense or marijuana. Most likely, one sees images of bright clothing, love beads, psychedelic art, rock concerts and political demonstrations. To many living in the 1980s, the 1960s seem to be a historical curiosity, a short-lived experiment in the extravagant, the exotic and the bizarre. Certainly, it might be argued that the flower people have gone to seed; "hippies" are no longer hip. Their time has passed.

But has it really? By charting what happened in the 1960s, we will find clues to the meaning of the New Age. We may even find that the counterculture is bidding, in a new and more persuasive way, to become the dominant culture.

The sixties' counterculture offered people a doorway into the new and the untried. The "business as usual" of American life had lost its life, they claimed. The "square" mind was enslaved by the demands of a despirited world of technology and materialism. Secularism had paralyzed the spiritual imagination and nailed shut the doors of the soul. The apollonian attitude of hard work, restraint and disciplined achievement (or the work ethic) left the counterculture cold. Instead they celebrated the dionysian ideal: the exuberant experiences beyond the mundane and predictable.

## The Making of a Counterculture

The Vietnam War, racial injustice and problems with the economy caused masses of students and young people to challenge the prevalent political order of the day in favor of a Neo-Marxist "New Left," ideologically fueled by the thought of Herbert Marcuse and others. The rock music of the era helped galvanize the political protests and expressed the new spiritual concerns of a post-Christian culture.

Stemming from the beatnik generation of the fifties, the counterculture questioned the traditional answers of American culture. Like their rebellious predecessors, but in much greater numbers, those in the counterculture explored the options of an increasingly pluralistic society. As the beat generation had flirted with Zen and all things Easterly exotic, so did the counterculture import Eastern religions and adjust them for the West. Hinduism came with a splash during the mid 1960s when the transcendental movement led by Maharishi Mahesh Yogi began to propagate Eastern metaphysics in terms of Western psychology and science. Various sects and cults dotted the countercultural landscape, setting up their own "alternative altars." Hare Krishnas chanted; assorted yogis, gurus and swamis promised enlightenment; and a generation became accustomed to non-Christian spiritual beliefs and practices. Both the sedentary spirituality of a dormant church and the materialism of an exhausted secular humanism were brought to account by a "new consciousness."

Other essential elements of the counterculture were hallucinogenic drugs and the revival of the occult. Following the lead of visionary intellectuals such as Aldous Huxley and Timothy Leary, a generation sought to raise its consciousness through both organic and synthetic drugs. Rather than traversing the long road of ascetic discipline and spiritual mastery known for millennia in the East, modern Americans sought cosmic consciousness by way of chemical expediency.

Many left the comfortable confines of straight society after experiencing other realities through drugs. Carlos Castaneda's popular books about his adventures with Don Juan sold millions of copies and helped make sorcery palatable to modern tastes. These stories of the mysterious Mexican sorcerer Don Juan attracted many who followed his path of initiation through the experience of hallucinogenic mushrooms.

Marilyn Ferguson credits the psychedelic movement of the sixties as being pivotal in the later development of the New Age movement. Speaking of "entry points" into the New Age movement, she mentions the "intense alternative reality generated by a psychedelic drug" and the impossibility of "overestimating the historic role of psychedelics as an entry point drawing people into other transformational technologies."[1] The Beatles, for instance, influenced millions by fusing hallucinogenic experience, Eastern philosophy and political dissent in the themes of many of their songs.

The occult influence on the counterculture can be seen in its announcement of itself as the "Age of Aquarius," an astrological term for the present age. Astrology is based on a monistic philosophy and is one of the most ancient occult arts (*occult* means "secret" or "hidden"). Forms of occult divination such as Tarot card reading and the *I Ching* along with mediumism, psychic encounters of all stripes and even Satanism, all contributed to make the counterculture an occult hotbed. Parapsychology labored to give scientific credibility to supernatural or occult phenomena such as precognition, clairvoyance, telekinesis and so on.

Our purpose is not to chronicle the counterculture but to chart its significance for the New Age. To deem the counterculture as but a passing trend is a serious error; for although many of the outward forms of its protest have receded from our cultural memory, many of its deepest claims have simply changed costume and are now becoming regular aspects of modern culture. What was open and irregular in the sixties—the "love-ins," "happenings," Eastern religious disciplines, occultism—became less ostentatious and quite well integrated into the general culture by the mid 1970s and on into the 1980s. The "*counter*culture" is seeking to become, as one New Age writer puts it, the "rising culture."

## The Demise of Secular Humanism

Before discussing the assimilation of the One into our everyday experience, we need to understand the failure of secular humanism and the counterculture's basic complaint against modern Western society. Secular humanism grew out of the religious humanism of the Renaissance. Having begun with a basically Christian appreciation of humanity, humanism progressively focused more attention on the glory of humanity, to the exclusion of the glory of God. Its world view shifted from theism to atheism. Human reason and scientific innovation became the final authority for life and thought, replacing God's revelation. Humanity became autonomous.

But for all its optimism concerning the freedom from religious superstition and outworn authority, secular humanism's world view contained fatal flaws. With God evacuated, the universe lost its ultimate purpose, meaning and value. Human beings were no longer seen as being made in the image of God but merely as the products of chance evolutionary forces. Morality was severed from its absolute, universal reference to God; instead it was determined by the whims of humanity—relativism.

Sensitive thinkers began to feel the price exacted by atheism. Some realized that secular humanism could easily degenerate into nihilism—the belief that everything is meaningless and absurd. Bertrand Russell even goes so far as to applaud this move:

That man is the product of causes which had no prevision of the end they were achieving; that his origin, his growth, his hopes and fears, his loves and his beliefs, are but the outcome of accidental collocations of atoms; that no fire, no heroism, no intensity of thought and feeling, can preserve an individual life beyond the grave; that all the noonday brightness of human genius, are destined to extinction in the vast death of the solar system, and that the whole temple of man's achievement must inevitably be buried underneath the debris of a universe in ruins—all these things, if not quite beyond dispute, are yet so nearly certain that no philosophy that rejects them can hope to stand. Only the scaffolding of these truths, only on the firm foundation of unyielding despair, can the soul's habitation be safely built.[2]

Despite Russell's assertion, no culture is long able to survive on a steady diet of atheism. Because we are made in the image of God, we seek transcendent meaning, purpose and value. Nihilism is unpalatable because it is unlivable. This "firm foundation of unyielding despair" is not congenial to the human spirit.

Despite several attempts, secular humanism has been unable to develop a durable or compelling world view. The acids of its own assumptions ruthlessly corrode its credibility and appeal. No matter what secular humanists like Carl Sagan and Isaac Asimov may do to glorify their chance universe, the philosophical dynamic of secular humanism seems close to the exhaustion point. Ideologically, it has yet to lose its grip; yet the logic of its resulting nihilism can do nothing but weaken its power.[3] While it appeals to humanity's quest for autonomy and crowns "man the measure of all things," we find ourselves the lords of nothing—nothing but a meaningless universe with no direction, destiny or purpose. Humanity becomes only an accidental upsurge of personality awaiting cosmic oblivion. The world which was once "charged with the grandeur of God" (Gerard Manley Hopkins) now becomes "a tale told by an idiot, full of sound and fury, signifying nothing" (Shakespeare).

## The Counterculture's Complaint

The counterculture's critique of Western secular humanism was as hostile in many ways as the Christian critique. Analysts such as Theodore Roszak locate the sources of our current distress in the great social transformations of the Scientific and Industrial Revolutions. With the advent of scientific experimentation and quantification, especially through the development of mathematics by Descartes and Galileo, the modern West began to desacralize the world. What was once the theater of mystic splendor and spiritual participation was slowly transformed into a cold mechanism of natural laws and regularities. The spirits were chased from the woods and only the trees remained. The sacred grove became the lumberyard as nature was viewed as mere stuff to be technologically utilized by the newfound powers of humanity come of age. The world was reduced to its essential physical components, that which could be touched, tasted, weighed or seen: the measurable. Eventually, with the development of scientism—secular humanism's belief that science alone is the source of truth and progress—whatever could not be measured was considered nonexistent or at least unimportant. The "real world" became the world of science and reason freed from religious superstition.

Although Christianity and the counterculture share some of the same criticisms of secular humanism, Roszak indicts Christianity as setting the wheels of secularism in motion. He believes that Christian theism degenerated into secular atheism because of its presuppositions about God, man and the world. If God is transcendent and distinct from the world, Roszak argues, the world is consequently divested of spiritual significance. In Christianity "nature is pronounced dead and desacralized."[4] This implicit dualism alienates the world from God, man from God, and man from the world and other men.

The organic harmony of all being, which Roszak calls "the old Gnosis" (alias, the One), is thus fragmented. The glories of the old "essentially magical world view" show a world pulsating with divine life and energy, in which divine vitality is experienced within the self and is not dependent on faith or doctrine. Christianity, and Protestantism in particular, destroyed this harmony.[5]

Thus Christianity contains the seeds of its own destruction and is to be directly blamed for the development of secular humanism and consequently for many modern ills. Its God was so distant that man forgot him entirely and was left to his own devices. Nature became a testing ground for man's technological devices, and the door was opened to untold technological carnage: the dehumanization of man and the pollution of the environment.

## The Rise of the One

As one of the counterculture's first apologists and prophets, Roszak scrutinized the West's political, economic, social and spiritual difficulties in terms of an incorrect world view that must be overthrown. He and others gave intellectual fiber to the movement that would last beyond the death of the externals of the hippie culture. Roszak's vision, much influenced by William Blake and the Eastern religions, was one of wholeness, imagination and a new view of nature. He argued that the dualisms of Christianity and secular humanism must be eradicated so that all reality may be seen and experienced as it truly is, as one. An overly mental faith in history and doctrine must be replaced by an inner experience of truth through the raising of consciousness. The wasteland of modern culture ends at the counterculture.

Cultural historian William Irwin Thompson likewise protested against the ravages of secularism and advocated animism as a way of resacralizing a barren earth. Better the enchanted world of spirits than the lifeless bulk of a meaningless universe. So we see that just when the spiritual was thought to be banished, it came back with pantheistic insistence.

Modern American pluralism gave the counterculture room to integrate itself into the fabric of society. Given time and sufficient intellectual development, even many extreme groups eventually find their way into the mainstream of culture. Christian Science, for example, was once considered an outlandish, heretical teaching on the fringe of America's religious consciousness. Now, one hundred years later, its schools, magazines, journals, churches and diversified groups of followers testify to its cultural staying power and assimilation.

America's religious freedom provides a fertile medium for alternative beliefs. The very presence of a dizzying variety of religious claims makes each claim more socially acceptable and, at the same time, makes each less comprehensively credible; that is, the belief in absolute truth is replaced by one's "religious preference." Although preference is not the same as certainty, if more and more of the myriad options of pluralism converge at the feet of the One, the "religious preference" for pantheism will sociologically solidify into a majority's certainty. And as we shall see and as the New Age claims, there are many ways to the One.

The radicalism and enthusiastic protest of the 1960s gave way to a more articulate and integrated view that developed in the 1970s. As the rest of the book will demonstrate, superficial extremism was replaced by a rethinking of the theoretical underpinnings of one Western intellectual discipline after another. The "movement" went from the streets to the libraries, studies and university classrooms. In speaking of mass movements, Eric Hoffer says that they "do not usually rise until the prevailing order has been discredited. The discrediting is not an automatic result of the blunders and abuses of those in power, but the deliberate work of men of words with a grievance."[6]

Men of words are moving toward the One. Having been exposed to Eastern spirituality and philosophy in the 1960s, grown-up hippies entering general culture often did not outgrow their pantheistic outlook; they simply accommodated to certain social conventions. Why worry about keeping long hair providing you can keep your world view? In fact, why not join the culture and permeate it from within instead of trying to tear it down through violent protest? Instead of quoting the Buddha or the Hindu Scriptures, why not write books and teach classes from an Eastern perspective? Instead of only practicing yoga or doing transcendental meditation yourself, why not try to implement it in the wider culture? Rather than "dropping out" like the beatniks or "freaking out" like the hippies, why not out*think* the "square" or "straight" culture?

Many singed by the extremes of the 1960s regrouped in the 1970s without fundamentally altering their ideals or views. They turned inward in hope of personal transformation. Jerry Rubin, radical "yippie" and dynamo for countercultural revolution, wrote in the midseventies of "growing up at 37." The inarticulate outcry against decadent American values did not give him personal peace or a whole vision of society. In disarray he temporarily retreated from his political radicalism to experience the New Consciousness in a number of manifestations from rolfing to est. Having become well acquainted with the One within, Rubin is optimistic for the future of the New Consciousness movement: "We are headed for another 'do it' period. Perhaps the 1980s will see the activism of the sixties combined with the awareness of the seventies. In the next flurry of activity we will come from a deeper psychological and spiritual base."[7]

No line can properly be drawn between the New Age movement and the counterculture, although differences can be seen. In addition to the fact that the New Age movement has become more sophisticated and has expanded its influence into the general culture, we can see that it is more than primarily a youth movement. People of all ages are involved. Second, many of those now involved in the New Age movement were not involved in the counterculture. Third, hardrock music is not as much of a rallying point as it was for the counterculture. In fact, a New Age style of music is developing which combines jazz, electric and meditative elements. Representative musicians are Kitaro and Stephen Halpern. Fourth, the emphasis on "free sex" has been somewhat tamed, although there has not been a return to traditional morality. Fifth, such practices as meditation and hypnosis are now used to "alter consciousness," rather than the more chemically severe hallucinogenics (LSD, peyote and others).[8]

Nevertheless the New Age apologetic and ideology builds on the counterculture's foundation while substantially expanding its conceptual cogency. What began as a scattered revolt against Western secularism and traditional Christianity has matured into an elaborate and full-orbed assault on Western culture. But it is more than an assault; it is a proposal for conquest. New Age advocates believe that the failure of secular humanism and the rejection of Christian theism has left us with a crisis: the megatonnage of nuclear terror threatens to vaporize us; our politics are pathetic; our spirituality is run-down and close to expiration; our economics border on world collapse. Transformation is required, and there is no going back. We face the turning point.

## The Appeal of Hope

Compelling social movements don't come by spontaneous generation. Various factors must be set in place for a challenging idea to capture the mind, heart and will of a society. First, a strong sense of foreboding and dread must impel the desire to change. Second, the present must be judged inadequate to meet modern needs. Third, a convincing appeal must be made for a forgotten tradition to come to the rescue. Fourth, hope in the future must be kindled and burn hotly at the very heart of the movement. The failure of secular humanism has caused the first two factors to come about. The New Age movement is trying to meet the second two.

A key ingredient in the appeal of the New Age is the hope for personal and social *transformation.* The appetite for transformation may be whetted by reflecting on the state of society or by a personal experience or a combination of both. We have already discussed the widespread disenchantment with modern Western materialism and technology that sparked the counterculture. The same discontent continues to spark the New Age movement. Madison Avenue can't fulfill the mystical longings of the soul; neither can mere material comforts or status satisfy the person in search of meaning and self-validation.

In today's world there are a variety of ways by which people's world views are challenged and they are introduced to a new dimension of reality. Marilyn Ferguson gives a list of the most popular of these experiences. All of them involve an increased "consciousness of one's consciousness"[9] and a rethinking of one's fundamental understanding of reality.

☐ Sensory isolation or overload.

☐ Biofeedback, a technique using devices that permit the individual to monitor and regulate his or her own brain waves.

☐ Creative activities such as painting, sculpting.

☐ Overwhelming aesthetic experience: music, theater, art.

☐ The consciousness-raising strategies of various social movements that call attention to old assumptions.

☐ Self-help groups such as AA or Overeaters Anonymous which stress "higher powers" that must be consulted.

☐ Hypnosis and self-hypnosis.

☐ All types of meditation: Zen, Tibetan Buddhist, chaotic, transcendental, esoteric Christian, cabalist, various types of yoga and others.

☐ Consciousness-changing seminars such as est, Lifespring and Silva Mind Control.

☐ Consciousness-changing devices such as Zen koans (paradoxical sayings), Sufi stories, dervish dancing, shamanistic and magical rituals to change awareness, fantasy games such as Dungeons and Dragons.

☐ Exploration into one's dream life; interest in Jungian analysis.

☐ Various therapies such as primal therapy, Gestalt, Arica and

rebirthing.
- ☐ Interest in martial arts: T'ai Chi Ch'uan, aikido, karate.
- ☐ Body disciplines such as rolfing, bioenergetics, Feldendrais, applied kinesiology.
- ☐ Feelings of self-transcendence and power experienced unexpectedly or in sports; Maslow's peak experiences.[10]

Concerning these kinds of experiences, Ferguson comments: "All of these approaches might be called _psychotechnologies_—systems for a deliberate change in consciousness. Individuals may independently discover a new way of paying attention and may learn to induce such states by methods of their own devising. Anything can work."[11]

Besides these entry points, a number of other concerns may propel people toward the One:

_Ecology._ Convinced by the criticisms of Roszak, Capra and others, many blame Christianity for the present ecological crisis. They believe that a God distinct and separate from nature can do little to insure the sacred quality of nature. Nothing less than the oneness of all things—god, man and nature—can insure a whole and balanced view of the natural environment. The modern mentality—Christian or otherwise—that objectifies and disenchants nature must be discarded before we are engulfed in an unsolvable ecological catastrophe. In this instance, Mother Earth replaces Father God.

_Feminism._ For Capra the idea of an overbearing male Deity gives license for men to rule over women and nature. The male God in heaven is both exclusivistic and distant. Many who are frustrated with the inequities of sexism turn toward a spiritual feminism that promises a more equitable and peaceful world view. People are re-exploring the maternal ground of all being, which emphasizes the feminine in nature and ethics—the nurturing, intuitive and subjective aspects of life that Western society has neglected or rejected.

_Authority._ Having been seduced and abandoned by secular humanism and disappointed in the results of scientism, many post-Christian sojourners yearn for some sense of authority on which to build their lives. The dilemma of spiritual overchoice burdens many. With secularization came the breakup of one generally agreed-on spiritual view of the world, or "plausibility structure." Now a myriad of options confront the spiritual aspirant, and he or she is likely to become "a very nervous Prometheus."[12] Consequently, many turn toward New Age ideologies in an attempt to regain a sense of bearing that only comes from following an established authority and unified world view.

The New Age world view derives much of its authority and appeal from a long line of pantheistic traditions. Ferguson notes that "the emergence of the Aquarian Conspiracy in the late twentieth century is rooted in the myths, metaphors, the prophesy and poetry of the past."[13] The pantheistic heritage runs long and deep, touching or permeating one culture after another since the dawn of recorded history. Thus the New Age draws inspiration and insight from an ancient consciousness. The One entices and enamors the modern mind since it is seen as a resurgence of a lost wisdom suppressed by secular humanism and Christianity. No one has summarized the perennial influence of pantheism better than C. S. Lewis:

> Pantheism is congenial to our minds not because it is the final stage in a slow process of enlightenment, but because it is almost as old as we are. . . . It is immemorial in India. The Greeks rose above it only at their peak, in the thought of Plato and Aristotle; their successors relapsed into the great Pantheistic system of the Stoics. Modern Europe escaped it only while she remained predominantly Christian; with Giordano Bruno and Spinoza it returned. With Hegel it became almost the agreed philosophy of highly educated people, while the more popular Pantheism of Wordsworth, Carlyle and Emerson conveyed the same doctrine to those on a slightly lower cultural level. So far from being the final religious refinement, Pantheism is in fact the permanent natural bent of the human mind. . . . It is the attitude into which the human mind automatically falls when left to itself.[14]

Add to this list the American, pantheistically oriented movements of Mind Cure/New Thought, Christian Science, Theosophy and Spiritualism in the nineteenth century and we find a rich vein of non-Christian spirituality from which to mine.

*Hope.* Despite secular humanism's advance in the modern world, it is a wounded warrior suffering from the fatal blow of philosophical consumption. Its own presuppositions rip it to shreds and prove ultimately suicidal. Existentialism's forceful but futile attempt to salvage meaning in a meaningless world was secular humanism's last real hope. Now hope shifts away from the floundering juggernaut. We now hear: experience the One; believe in the One; hope in the One.

Man cannot live long without hope. With secular humanism at the end of its tether, a replacement is mandatory. As Morris Berman states:

> For more than 99 percent of human history, the world was enchanted and man saw himself as an integral part of it. The complete reversal of this perception in a mere four hundred years or so has destroyed the continuity of the human experience and the integrity of the human psyche. It has very nearly wrecked the planet as well. The only hope, or so it seems to me, lies in the re-enchantment of the world.[15]

Berman views modern secular humanism as a pox on all existence. We must transcend the error of the present age by learning from the "enchanted" past and hoping for a "re-enchanted future." As Eric Hoffer has said, "There is no more potent dwarfing of the present than by viewing it as a mere link between a glorious past and a glorious future."[16]

The "only hope," according to Berman, is the return of the One. If the modern Western mind is but a historical aberration, a rationalistic abnormality of recent invention, it can be overcome and replaced. We must look forward in order to be strengthened and encouraged. Hoffer says, "No faith is potent unless it is also faith in the future; unless it has a millennial component. So, too, an effective doctrine:

as well as being a source of power, it must also claim to be a key to the book of the future."[17]

Visionaries such as Teilhard de Chardin and Sri Aurobindo prophesied a New Consciousness to surpass even past experience of the One for all. Teilhard spoke of the "Omega point" and Aurobindo of the "Supermind" that will usher in planetary consciousness. Maharishi Mahesh Yogi, the leader of transcendental meditation, speaks of a coming age of enlightenment. Peter Russell, in his book *The Global Brain,* speaks of the "increasing pace of evolution" and the potential for amazing change. Our present crisis will serve as an evolutionary catalyst to push us forward.

> Evolutionary trends and patterns . . . suggest a further possibility: the emergence of something beyond a single planetary consciousness or Supermind: a completely new level of evolution, as different from consciousness as consciousness is from life, and life is from matter.[18]

According to many New Age thinkers evolution has become conscious of itself in humanity. Our role is to take evolution into our own hands and reshape ourselves for the betterment of all humanity. We have no choice but to advance. Barbara Marx Hubbard even views the atom bomb as an "evolutionary driver" that will force the nations to cooperate and eventually see themselves as one in the One.[19] As she says, "crisis precedes transformation"[20] and makes it necessary.

But if the transformation is to be complete, it must permeate and overtake the Western mindset. This means nothing less than the infiltration and revision of the major intellectual disciplines as well as the common world view of the person on the street. The One must move from the avant-garde fringe to the very heart and mind of society. And this is exactly what is happening. The often laughable cosmic claptrap of the sixties has been replaced by a more mature and compelling world view that seeks to draw all areas of life into its confidence.

## Cosmic Humanism

As the "rising culture" of New Age thought overtakes the culture of secular humanism, we see that the impetus for the transition is generated from within the present culture rather than forced on it from without. The New Age and secular humanism are more like cousins than strangers, and the competition between the two world views is more of an in-house feud than a dispute between opposites. A better metaphor might be to view the One as taking the baton from a once robust but now failing secular humanism so that the race to win Western civilization might be won by a new kind of humanism—cosmic humanism.

The origin of modern humanism in the Renaissance and Enlightenment was closely related to pantheism, occultism and animism. Connections with the supernatural were not immediately severed when Christianity was challenged, redefined or overthrown. The spiritual emphasis simply switched from God's glory to humanity's. Pantheistic humanists such as Pico della Mirandola and later Giordano Bruno affirmed the immanence of God and denied the distinction between Creator and creation. According to Ernst Cassirer, Bruno helped radically transform the West's view of nature. For him nature "is elevated to the sphere of the divine."[21]

*Manas,* a New Age oriented periodical, comments that "the heart of classical Humanism . . . is [the] joint principle of freedom and responsible self-reliance in the nature of man."[22] Freedom meant freedom from Christian doctrine and from the idea that we need to be redeemed by a God external to ourselves. *Manas* continues, "Man is no sinful worm, but potential divinity." Cassirer comments that reconciliation between God and humanity "was no longer looked for exclusively in an act of divine grace; it was supposed to take place amid the activity of the human spirit and its process of self-development."[23] This "potential divinity" (the One within) is the human nature that early humanism strove to actualize.

After the Scientific Revolution, humanism became secular in that it began to restrict human nature to the rational and analytical powers. Skepticism of the supernatural and the divine replaced the belief in the divine within. According to *Manas,* any humanism that neglects the "higher will" (divine potential) is a "denatured humanism," hardly on a par with the past greatness of Pico or Bruno.[24]

Yet even denatured humanism has much in common with earlier humanism and the coming cosmic humanism. First of all, secular humanism and the philosophy of the One (pantheism) affirm that there is but one reality. For secular humanism all is matter and energy arranged by chance. Carl Sagan declares in his best-selling book *Cosmos* (also a television series) that "the Cosmos is all that is or ever was or ever will be."[25] In essence, secular humanism has a monism of matter and energy, while cosmic humanism (the One) has a monism of spirit—all is god.

Our salvation, for the secular humanist, comes through rational inquiry and the development of science. *Humanist Manifesto II* (1973) affirms that "no deity will save us; we must save ourselves." It goes on to say that "reason and intelligence are the most effective instruments that humankind possesses." Our hope lies in the nature of man and his potential. "Saving ourselves" for the signers of the first *Humanist Manifesto* (1933) meant "the complete realization of human personality."[26] The new cosmic humanism essentially agrees but expands the territory. Man is not only the measure of all things, he is the metaphysical master; we are one with the One and thus have access to unlimited potential.

The materialism of secular humanism is being usurped by the mysticism of the One. Yet both look to humanity for the answer, not to anything outside of us. Whereas the old humanism says we are "naked apes"—the product of chance evolution—the new cosmic humanism sees us as gods in disguise. Brooks Alexander insightfully describes this change:

Occult philosophy is humanism taken to its logical conclusion. Occult philosophy, like its secular cousin, takes humanity as the source and center of meaning, but defines humanity as the manifestation of deity and thereby inflates it to cosmic dimensions. Humanity becomes so amplified and self-sufficient that God is excluded. His functions are simply absorbed.[27]

Once secular humanism becomes independent from the supernatural and theological, it naturally gravitates back to the One—irrepressibly and inescapably. Pantheism is, as C. S. Lewis said, the permanent natural bent of the human mind.

The key problem for the secular humanist is the genesis of mind in the universe. How can mere matter in motion produce mind? How can inanimate chance give birth to animate purposeful beings such as animals and people? Lifeless matter could never transcend itself. Thus philosophical evolutionists asserted that consciousness emerged from the latent potentialities in matter.[28] Matter is not lifeless but spiritually potent. This latent consciousness (mind) becomes actualized in evolution and conscious of itself in man. The difficulty of matter producing mind disappears, but what is left is more than materialistic humanism, as theologian Charles Hodge noted a century ago:

> If you only spiritualize matter until it becomes mind, the absurdity disappears. And so does materialism, and spontaneous generation, and the whole array of scientific doctrines. If matter becomes mind, mind is God, and God is everything. Thus the monster Pantheism swallows up science and its votaries.[29]

Quite naturally, then, "materialism evolves into pantheism."[30]

Probably no nation has been more ideologically and institutionally atheistic than the Soviet Union. The official Marxist world view admits nothing but "matter in motion" as the ultimate reality. God and the supernatural have been jettisoned from its ideological universe as pious excuses for social oppression.

Yet here too secular humanism may be expanding its boundaries to include the paranormal. In an interview in *New Age* magazine, Michael Murphy describes the new spiritual climate he discovered in the U.S.S.R. as "a cultural awakening . . . not unlike the awakening in America in the 1960s."[31] He says that "what unites it all is a growing conviction among many Soviet citizens and scientists that hidden human reserves must be discovered and developed."[32] "Hidden human reserves" refers to the innate paranormal powers of man. The effort is being made to reconcile these powers with Marxist dogma.

Murphy claims that Russians' spiritual heritage is again bursting forth after years of political repression. But the resurgence is not Christian; it is essentially pantheistic. He comments that "thousands of Soviet citizens are reading books by Fritz Perls, Carlos Castaneda, John Lilly, and Abraham Maslow. Literature in yoga, Sufism, Buddhism, Vedanta, Kabbalah, the lost knowledge of ancient civilizations, and other esoteric subjects is available and finds a wide audience."[33] The above authors and schools of thought are all prophets of the One for all. Whereas traditional Marxism limited the One to the material, a new synthesis struggles to emerge that would extend the realms of the natural to include the extraordinary. The "divine within" seeps into the structures even of atheism, which is hardly surprising since humanity has always been its god anyway. Materialism is not central to humanism; it is simply a suit of clothes to be worn or shorn, depending on the social climate. What is essential is human-centeredness, the One for all and in all.

We are seeing the entrance of what C. S. Lewis called "the materialist magician"[34]—the nontheist who believes in what has traditionally been called the "supernatural." But, we must remember that according to *Humanist Manifesto II* "nature may be broader and deeper than we now know."[35] So the supernatural is not really supernatural, but another dimension of the natural.

## Pluralism and the One

The God within is the One for all. But how, in our pluralistic society, can *One* (only one) be for *all*? Doesn't pluralism mean a variety of beliefs held in the same society at the same time?

The situation may superficially appear more like polytheism (many gods) than monism (the One). Yet while the sheer number of philosophical and religious options in society serves to weaken the credibility of them all (how can we know which one is really true?), a society filled with doubt will not stand without finding a new consensus. The pantheon of gods now reigning must fight for supremacy; gods tolerate no equals. Although a throng of gods come rushing in to fill the void left by the decline of Christianity and secular humanism, more than a mere throng is needed for social stability and direction. As Mircea Eliade has said, secular man "killed a God in whom he could not believe but whose absence he could not bear."[36] The pluralism we now experience is fragmented and confused. The rootlessness and ambiguity of modern pluralism may serve as a goad for a new unified and unifying consensus. Edward Norman speculates that *pluralism* "is a word society employs during the transition from one orthodoxy to another. . . . A society cannot remain permanently fragmented with respect to values."[37] Our brand of pluralism may prove to be more of a provisional tolerance of divergent ideas than a permanent smorgasbord of beliefs. It may well begin to collapse as its inner tensions pull it apart. But what else may emerge?

Are we on the verge of a new orthodoxy, a new climate of opinion dominated by the One? Some fervently hope so. And some fear so. By inflating human potential to cosmic dimensions, cosmic humanism has captured much of secular humanism without being ensnared by its narrow, repressive elements. It takes the torch from the failing runner. Brooks Alexander puts it well: "Cosmic Humanism has come in at an appropriate point to infuse and spiritualize secularism, catalytically transforming it into an agency for the transmission of ultimate values. In that way it becomes a force of social cohesion rather than dissolution."[38]

In the following chapters, the infiltration of this "new orthodoxy" into the areas of health, psychology, science, politics and spirituality will be charted and analyzed to see if the One is truly "for all "

# Holistic
# Health

**3**

THROUGHOUT HISTORY HEALTH HAS BEEN A MUCH-PRIZED BUT ELUSIVE possession of humanity. Shamans, priests, doctors and other healers have all sought to cure our perennial sicknesses, using all manner of treatments—from exorcisms to incisions. Yet the ills of the body continue to frustrate the will of the mind. We want health and deliverance from decay and death, but our bodies stubbornly follow another course.

Today *holistic* health (taken from the Greek word *holos,* meaning "whole") is bringing new hope for healing to many. Its goal is to treat not only the sickness but the whole person—body, mind and spirit. With its new philosophy of medicine and health it is exploding many of the old assumptions of traditional medical practice.

Holistic health practitioners see modern Western medicine as reductionistic. It has lost its holistic vision and, consequently, reduces persons to mere bodies—machinelike assemblages of separable parts. Disease is viewed as a mechanistic malfunction remedied by chemical or surgical intervention. Spiritual concerns are banished from health considerations altogether.

The health professions' mechanistic view of people, rising malpractice suits, dangerous prescription drugs, iatrogenic (doctor-caused) illnesses and soaring costs have caused more and more people to question modern medicine. Many would agree with Voltaire's evaluation: "Physicians pour drugs of which they know little, to cure diseases of which they know less, into humans of which they know nothing."[1] Discontent with establishment medicine coupled with a gnawing feeling of helplessness in the face of death and disease has brought many to the purported healing fount of holistic health.

But is holistic health the panacea its advocates claim it to be? While many aspects of the movement are helpful and corrective, most practices are based on pantheistic or New Age philosophy. Whether employing the ancient way of Chinese acupuncture or the modern technique of biofeedback, the goal of holistic health practice is often said to be to attune one with the One.

Marilyn Ferguson is enthusiastic about the concept of holistic health, seeing it as "legitimized by federal and state programs, endorsed by politicians, urged and underwritten by insurance companies, co-opted in terminology (if not always in practice) by many physicians, and adopted by medical students."[2] A trip to a local health-food store will probably reveal a score of books covering Chinese medicine, self-hypnosis, macrobiotics, biofeedback, meditation and other practices billed as restoring the whole person. But just what is holistic health? Can Christians learn from it or must it be rejected?

## Ten Dominant Themes

Although holistic health is not now a unified approach or movement, Paul and Teri Reisser and John Weldon have put together ten dominant themes that characterize its adherents.[3] I should add that not

all practitioners of the "New Medicine" follow all ten of these pre-
cepts; nor do I want to imply that believing in one or some of these
ideas labels one automatically a disciple of the New Age movement.
Nevertheless these themes give an accurate summary of New Age
health care.

1. *The whole is greater than the parts.* Humans are fully integrated
wholes who cannot be treated as biological machines. Capra criticizes what he calls the modern "biomedical model" for "concentrating
on smaller and smaller fragments of the body" and so "losing sight
of the patient as a human being."[4] The human being is more than a
cellular and molecular mechanism, and to focus on these processes
to the exclusion of the whole person is medical tunnel vision. Bodily
malfunction should not be abstracted from a person's diet, environment and mental attitude, since they all contribute to the total picture.

2. *Health or "wellness" is more than an absence of disease.* Capra
comments that "although medicine has contributed to the elimina-
tion of certain diseases, this has not necessarily restored health."[5]
Optimum health goes beyond the absence of disease to include the
well-being of the whole person in every area. Health or wellness is
a positive state of growth and self-realization. Many within the movement would agree with Andrew Weil's definition of health as "a dynamic and harmonious equilibrium of all elements and forces making
up and surrounding a human being."[6]

3. *We are responsible for our own health or disease.* Holistic health
insists that individuals reclaim their bodies from the tyranny of the
medical establishment. Rather than passively submit to the scientific
gnosis of the medical elite, people must actively pursue their own
health. Establishment medicine's monopoly must be broken. Capra
objects to the "mystique that surrounds the medical profession"
which causes us to confer "on physicians the exclusive right to determine what constitutes illness, who is sick and who is well, and
what should be done to the sick."[7] Ferguson refers to the innate

healing power of the body when she quotes an anatomist as saying that "the healer inside us is the wisest, most complex, integrated entity in the universe." She adds that we now know "there is always a doctor in the house."[8]

4. *Natural forms of healing are preferable to drugs and surgery.* Capitalizing on the detrimental effects of some modern medicine and the instances of unneeded surgeries, holistic health prefers less extreme methods of healing. Changes in diet, lifestyle and attitude should be explored in healing. Fearing that the "cure" of modern medicine may be worse than the problem, holistic health is suspicious of medical technology.

5. *Most methods of promoting health can be holistic, but some methods are more innately holistic than others.* Holistic health tends to question or disdain conventional medicine, claiming it is based on a faulty, mechanistic view of the person. (Yet even specialists may be holistic if they integrate their specialty with a concern for the whole person.) A number of alternative practices to Western medicine have become popular in recent years. Although not all are necessarily linked with New Age thought, all of them are regularly used by those in the movement. I will briefly describe some of the more popular techniques.

*Acupuncture, acupressure* and their modern derivatives seek to unblock and redirect energy flow through the insertion of needles (acupuncture) or use of pressure (acupressure) at key points on the body so as to balance healing energies.

*Biofeedback* is a technique that uses electrical monitoring of brain waves to bring normally unconscious, involuntary bodily functions under conscious, voluntary control. This may be extended to include altered states of consciousness and psychic experience.

*Chiropractic,* developed in the late nineteenth century by Daniel Palmer, locates the cause and correction of disease in the spine. Misalignment (or subluxations) of the spine are manipulated to restore health. *Osteopathy* does not restrict the manipulations to the spine but works with the whole body.

*Homeopathy* is a system founded by Samuel Hahneman (1755–1843) based on the idea that "like cures like." Small doses of substances considered harmful in larger doses are prescribed for healing. Weil notes that the amount of substances given is so infinitesimal that the homeopath believes it is not the material aspect of the drug that is efficacious but the spiritual aspect.[9]

*Iridology* is a form of diagnosis that considers the eyes to be windows of the body. The eye's iris is inspected for irregularities that signify disorders elsewhere in the body.

*Massage* and *body-work therapies* are designed to revitalize the body by releasing blocked energies through physical contact. Practices such as orgonomy, functional integration, zone therapy, rolfing, do'in, shiatsu, polarity therapy and bioenergetic analysis all in their own way seek to make us "physically healthier by invigorating our blood and lymph, by mending old muscle injuries or by putting our joints back into the shape that nature had in mind." They also try to "make us emotionally and perhaps psychically healthier" by making a " 'life force,' called 'ki' or 'prana' or 'innate intelligence' . flow more freely."[10]

Holistic health almost universally stresses the need for psychological peace through the practice of some form of Eastern *meditation.* This is thought to still the mind and release healing energy from within. Various books and therapies also urge people to use *visualization* or guided imagery to diagnose and heal illnesses. A positive mental image of a particular health problem will effect healing through the innate and often untapped power of consciousness. The same effect is sought through administered and self-*hypnosis.* An advocate of Eastern meditation, physician Larry Dossey believes the source of many modern stress-related diseases is actually an outdated view of space and time contradicted by modern physics. He feels that oriental mysticism is both more accurate and more helpful.[11] Various oriental *martial arts* such as karate, judo and aikido seek to use universal energy for self-defense and spiritual development.

As traditional, Western medicine, with its manmade chemical prescriptions, falls out of repute with many who seek healing, *nutritional therapies*—such as vitamin, herb and root therapies and cures—regain popularity. Because magazines that stress natural cures and preventatives, such as *Prevention,* sometimes feature articles on acupressure or TM, "the search for a new diet may end with a new world view as well."[12]

*Psychic diagnosis* and *psychic healing* are also becoming more popular. Reisser, Reisser and Weldon describe psychic diagnosis as "any technique in which information about a patient is obtained without using ordinary methods of questioning, examination and reproducible data."[13] This may include psychometry (diagnoses through holding an object owned by the person), clairvoyance and mediumistic or spiritistic diagnosis made through a "spirit guide." Shamans and traditional folk healers are also being greeted by some in the medical establishment. After describing two incidents where folk healers worked with traditional psychiatrists to effect unorthodox cures, a *Science Digest* article commented that "from Indian reservations to inner cities, evidence is accumulating that the worlds of the folk healer and the mental health professional can come together productively."[14] One folk healer with the aid of "her spirits" diagnosed the cause of a woman's schizophrenia. Michael Harner, an American anthropologist and practicing shaman, noted the similarities between shamanistic healing and some holistic health practices and concluded that "in a sense, shamanism is being reinvented in the West precisely because it is needed."[15]

As interest in Eastern religion proliferates so does interest in Eastern *sexual/mystical practices* that promise a fuller and healthier sex life. Various types of tantric yoga incorporate ritualized and extended forms of sexual intimacy as a vehicle to health and mystical enlightenment. *Yoga Journal* claims that couples who regularly practice tantra "describe a rapture that transports them beyond their ordinary selves.        Their limits and edges seem to dissolve; they merge into one being." They may also experience mystical visions.[16] George Leonard, long-time New Age activist, describes "the erotic encounter" as a "state of pure being" in which he can say, "I am as a god" and "I am not male, my love is not female. We are one, one entity."[17] Coupled with the libidinal explosion of the sexual revolution, tantra and other sexual therapies attract many.

6. *Health implies evolution.* As mentioned earlier, the New Age movement is aglow with messianic anticipations. Holistic health is seen by many as one manifestation of the advance into the New Consciousness and New Age. Jonas Salk, inventor of the polio vaccine, made this clear at a holistic health conference in 1977 when he spoke of "the historical, even evolutionary significance of the holistic health movement" which he anticipated would "facilitate the next stage in human evolution."[18]

7. *An understanding of energy, not matter, is the key to health.* The universal energy of which we are all a part is frequently cited as the source of healing. We are not clumps of dead matter but configurations of active energy. To increase the flow of healing energy we must attune ourselves to it and realize our unity with all things. In proposing a "space-time model" of health, Larry Dossey says that "the boundary of our physical self, our skin, is an illusion. It is no boundary at all."[19] Here we begin to see the One for all quite clearly. Many involved with holistic health adopt a pantheistic view of energy which maintains that "we are not just independent blobs of energy, but an intimate part of the universal energy, the creative force of the universe, the universal consciousness, whose energy flows through us and unites us."[20] While many in holistic health may wed this idea to modern physics to give it scientific credibility, the idea of God as impersonal, universal energy is ancient and has been called many names, such as *prana* and *kundalini* (Hindu), *mana* (used by Polynesian shamans) and *ch'i* (Taoism).[21]

8. *Death is the final stage of growth.* Although the quest for lon-

gevity is a passion for many in holistic health, death is often viewed as a transition to another state of consciousness or as an illusion. Hope for immortality has been sparked by Raymond Moody's book *Life after Life* and the books of Elizabeth Kübler-Ross which report the adventures of those who have supposedly died and lived to tell about it. Dossey says that the abandonment of a linear conception of time releases us from the fear of death and an ultimate end. He says that "death, in the new view of health, becomes effete." And because all is one, *individuals* cannot die. Dossey explains that since "all bodies are coextensive through concrete, dynamic, physical processes, the notion of individual death becomes absurd." Thus "we abandon death and its spectre of fear, suffering, and inexorable decline of life."[22]

9. *The thinking and practices of ancient civilizations are a rich source for healthy living.* Whether it be ancient shamanistic, Chinese or Indian cultures, holistic health looks to the past for wisdom. Pre-Christian and pretechnological cultures are seen as exemplars of holistic understanding and practice. As Reisser, Reisser and Weldon note, although the Bible is full of incidents of healing, holistic health usually avoids it as a source of wisdom because of its nonmonistic world view.[23]

10. *Holistic health must be incorporated into the fabric of society through public policy.* Ideas have political consequences, and holistic health adherents desire that its practices be implemented governmentally. Capra contends that both health education and health policies should follow the holistic model.[24] A Washington conference called "Holistic Health: A Public Policy" sponsored in 1978 by several government agencies, is but one example of governmental funds promoting holistic health. Ferguson notes that the topics included yoga, Buddhist meditation and assorted holistic health practices.[25]

**Holy or Holistic?**
The explosion of interest in the broad range of philosophies and

practices known as holistic health precludes easy and simple evaluation. Holistic health's concern to heal the gaping wound of modern medical incompetence is commendable. Social critic Ivan Illich has pointed out the detrimental effects of "the medicalization of society" which creates a radical monopoly in health. This monopoly is not only economic but psychological. Accompanying the rise of modern medicine has been the notion that only the medical elite are fit to heal. Illich summarizes this in terms of levels of *iatrogenesis*.

Iatrogenesis is clinical when pain, sickness, and death result from medical care; it is social when health policies reinforce an industrial organization that generates ill-health; it is cultural and symbolic when medically sponsored behavior and delusions restrict the vital autonomy of people by undermining their competence in growing up, caring for each other, and aging, or when medical intervention cripples personal responses to pain, disability, impairment, anguish, and death.[26]

Illich's critique of modern medical practices and their cultural impact drives us to consider alternative approaches and to question many established practices and philosophies. His thesis that "the medical establishment has become a major threat to health" is well documented and persuasively presented.[27] Yet a wholesale escape from modern medicine would be both foolish and unwarranted. What is needed is the best of modern medicine placed into a Christian context—medicine with a soul.

Historically healing has been naturally associated with religion. Despite this, modern medical-technological overkill and the view of healing as a business instead of a service has separated the spiritual from the physical. This has forced many into the open arms of holistic health. But what really awaits them?

Some of the ideas and practices of holistic health make positive contributions to surmounting the shortcomings of modern medicine. First, treating people as whole beings is eminently sound. The spiritual dimensions of healing should not be avoided. One's entire life and lifestyle contribute to one's health. We are more than machines and should be treated as such.

Second, the concept of positive "wellness" (instead of mere absence of disease) is appropriate. Christ called people to have life and have it more abundantly through him. This involves the whole person and an active advance into the adventure of living.

Third, people should take responsibility for their own health instead of passively placing the responsibility on doctors or drugs. Christians are called to glorify God in their bodies, which are the temples of the Holy Spirit (1 Cor 6:19).

Despite these positive aspects, the holism of much of holistic health is less than holy. While many involved in holistic health may not follow the idea that all is one and all is god, this is what is most often meant by *holistic*. The emphasis on "universal energy" betrays the world view. Although not all in the profession would agree, one chiropractor makes his views crystal clear: "The chiropractor believes that the innate intelligence that runs the body is connected to universal intelligence that runs the world, so each person is plugged into the universal intelligence through the nervous system."[28] Ancient Chinese medicine such as acupuncture and acupressure is intimately connected to Taoism, an essentially monistic world view. Acupuncture and acupressure are designed to stimulate and balance energy flow and so harmonize one with the One (or Tao).[29] Shamanistic and traditional folk healing are premised on an animistic or pantheistic view. Psychic and mediumistic healing is nothing but blatant, old-fashioned occultism.

Clearly, the Christian cannot condone a vision of health rooted in spiritual deception. Whatever the efficacy of these various practices, the Christian must be careful to test the spirits to uncover unbiblical ideas (1 Jn 4:1). Christians realize that the spiritual realm is real but not uniformly benevolent. A host of rebellious spirits or demons can masquerade as agents of healing and health for the purpose of diverting attention from the Great Physician.

Holistic health sometimes falls prey to the great lie that we are masters of our own destiny and lords of reality. While it is undoubtedly true that the Creator has wisely built into us natural processes of healing, we are all subject to moral and physical degeneracy because of sin. Holistic health tends to ignore the reality of the Fall and personal sinfulness and instead offers the hope of vibrant health and wholeness apart from reconciliation with a holy God through Jesus Christ.

Besides this, physical health and even emotional contentment is not synonymous with salvation. While salvation in Christ offers the restoration of wholeness (to be culminated in the world to come), health in itself is not the final goal. G. K. Chesterton observed that "those who worship health cannot remain healthy" and that "the glad good news brought by the Gospel was the news of original sin."[30] After recognizing sin, we may turn to the Savior. But in denying sin, we seek to be our own saviors. What Clifford Wilson and John Weldon say about occultism is also true for much of holistic health. "Occultists have always tried to deny and escape the effects of the Fall and to have mastery over the environment themselves, even the cosmos. Rather than *turn* to God, they wish to *become* him."[31]

The psychological and spiritual dangers of occult involvement in such practices as psychic healing have been well documented. They include insanity, demonic possession and other maladies.[32] Much of what purports to be holistic is often less than holy; it may result in the horrors of occult oppression. In disguising himself as an angel of light (2 Cor 11:14), Satan may hide his poisonous intent under the white robes of the mystic healer. But the poison remains.

A world-view analysis of holistic health is indispensable, but specific considerations must also enter the picture. Should Christians shun holistic health because some of its practices are based on a nonbiblical world view? This is not a simple issue. Non-Christian cultures have produced great works of art, science and literature that can be appreciated by Christians. The maxim "All truth is God's truth" should be taken seriously. Although all practices that smack of spiritism, mediumship or psychic manipulation should be avoided because of demonic involvement,[33] not all practices somehow associated with holistic health should be shunned. Biofeedback, for example, may simply be used to gain voluntary control of some bodily func-.ion.[34] But when it is used as a tool to supposedly raise one's consciousness to the divine level, it should be rejected. If any holistic practice has a questionable or non-Christian origin, it must be carefully evaluated to see if it inextricably involves unbiblical assumptions and/or practices. If so, it must be avoided.[35]

Hypnosis is often seen as a means to unblock psychic barriers and release healing energy. Yet Martin and Diedre Bobgan argue that it is based on psychological deception ("suggestion"), gives inordinate power to the hypnotist, is often connected with the occult and can have deleterious results.[36] Christians should therefore be well advised.

Another practice we should be cautious with is yoga. All forms of yoga involve occult assumptions, even *hatha* yoga, which is often presented as a purely physical discipline. Even advocates of yoga report the dangers of the energy *(kundalini)* it may awaken. This may involve insanity, physical burning, sexual abberations and so on. Although Paul says that physical discipline is of some use, we should steer clear of yoga.[37] Of course some beneficial physical exercise may resemble certain yoga practices. In this case the intention and spiritual condition of the person is important.

The medical effectiveness of practices such as acupuncture and acupressure is also a main consideration. Despite their recent popularity some researchers have found them to be less than miracle cure-alls. Medical research has yet to establish their efficacy or relation to any known processes of healing.[38] The idea of a universal life force or energy has also yet to correspond with modern medical knowledge and in fact may involve demonic forces.[39]

The rejection of standard medical practices may also open people to absurd and superstitious methods of diagnosis and treatment. Our desire to annul the realities of a fallen world often push us into the abyss of irrationalism. Although interested in many holistic practices, Andrew Weil is "bothered by the uncritical acceptance of unorthodox methods by doctors who call themselves holistic. . . . Medical practices are not sound just because they are unorthodox."[40] He specifically criticizes applied kinesiology, a method of determining organ weakness by testing muscles' resistance, and hair-shaft analysis (used by some naturopaths) as diagnostic tools since both are unscientific and easily abused.

According to a biblical and logical analysis, at its worst holistic health may be quackery, superstition or occultism. Let the buyer beware!

## Biblical Wholeness

Christians should be challenged by holistic health to explore the biblical dimensions of health and healing. Groups like The American Holistic Medical Association, The East-West Academy of the Healing Arts, The Mandala Society and The Association for Holistic Health are mounting a growing offensive. If Christians do not critically evaluate health issues and give informed responses, both in theory and in life, the One for all will gather more and more ground through holistic health.

The Old Testament offers many practical guidelines for health and sanitation. This is explained in S. I. McMillen's classic book, *None of These Diseases*.[41] A key but often neglected element of health is the importance of rest, found in the observation of the sabbath. Commenting that modern science has borne out the importance of rest once a week to avoid physical and mental breakdown, R. K. Harrison concludes that the "biblical concept of the sabbath has not merely positive and recuperative values for the individual but also serves to guard against disease."[42]

The Bible agrees with the New Age idea that one's mental attitude and consciousness affect health. Proverbs 3:7-8 says: "Do not be wise in your own eyes; fear the LORD and shun evil. This will bring health to your body and nourishment to your bones." The Christian ultimately looks to God for health and healing. As Christians cautiously scrutinize holistic health, they should not swing to the opposite extreme of placing uncritical confidence in modern medicine and be like King Asa of Israel who, though suffering from a severe illness, "did not seek help from the LORD, but only from the physicians" (2 Chron 16:12).

God may heal through natural processes or supernaturally through miracles. While the latter has often been either entirely neglected because of a lack of faith or abused by undiscerning zeal, God is a healing God (Ex 15:26), as the many healings of Jesus and the early church demonstrate. The church should rise to the New Age challenge with a deeper investigation of the healing ministry in all its dimensions.[43]

Yet whatever our physical condition may be, a loving God offers for us spiritual wholeness through faith. As the apostle Paul said: "Do not be anxious about anything, but in everything, by prayer and petition, with thanksgiving, present your requests to God. And the peace of God, which transcends all understanding, will guard your hearts and your minds in Christ Jesus" (Phil 4:6-7).

# Exploring Human
# Potential
# in Psychology

# 4

IN THE SECULARIZED WEST, PSYCHOLOGY HAS REPLACED THEOLOGY AS THE center of human concern. People are looking within to find answers to our modern anxieties. According to Martin Gross, we live in "the most anxious, emotionally insecure and analyzed population in the history of man"; we are "the citizens of the contemporary Psychological Society."[1] The Psychological Society is one "in which, as never before, man is preoccupied with *Self.*"[2]

In a pluralistic society the sheer bulk of belief-options serves to erode the credibility of any one option. Change seems inescapable. Whereas premodern societies were institutionally solid, if not monolithic, modern societies provide little philosophical or ideological stability. Everything seems up for grabs. People "do their own thing" and "have their own space." Consequently, pluralized people turn inward for direction and guidance, having abandoned the social structure as incapable of providing meaning. Peter Berger sums up the modern situation:

> The individual's experience of himself becomes more real to him than his experience of the objective social world. Therefore, the individual seeks to find his "foothold" in reality in himself rather than outside himself. One consequence of this is that the individual's subjective reality (what is commonly regarded as his "psychology") becomes increasingly differentiated, complex—and "interesting" to himself. Subjectivity acquires previously unconceived of "depths."[3]

When the social structures of meaning and value collapse, we turn within.

Yet the turn inward often results in a crisis of identity. Social roles are undefined or confusing. The world of the psyche has few road maps. The search within frequently falls short of the authenticity and assurance that is craved. This leads to anxiety and stress. Paul Rosch describes stress as "a chronic, relentless psychological situation" in modern society.[4] Stress is known to contribute to a host of illnesses, such as heart disease, cancer, lung ailments, accidental injuries, cirrhosis of the liver and suicide—six of the leading causes of death in the United States.[5] The Psychological Society is also the sick society and is calling out for help.

The New Consciousness offers itself as just that—a new mind, a new way of thinking and being. The help it offers is the answer within, a revitalized self seen for what it truly is: an unlimited source for growth and potential. An ad in *Science Digest* captures this spirit. Upon purchasing a new book on improving memory the buyer is promised, among other things, that he or she can discover "real ESP" by "using your mind correctly." We are also informed that "your mind has no limits." The book is but one of many therapies, training sessions and techniques designed to realize the hidden powers of the mind. In promising personal transformation, the New Age seeks to liberate the human mind, to provide a New Consciousness and psychology. Thus psychology becomes a main tributary for the One for all.

Before charting the leaning of modern psychology toward the New Consciousness, we will attend to the decline in traditional psychological theories and therapies.

## Freud and Company

Modern psychology came into its own with Sigmund Freud (1856-1939) and his psychoanalytic school. The psychoanalytic view of man has profoundly influenced how we see ourselves. Far more than simply a therapeutic technique, the Freudian world view has expanded into all areas of life.

Freud considered himself a great destroyer of false human traditions and assumptions. After over a century of confidence in the ability of the human intellect to discover truth, Freud sought to shine a light on this Enlightenment illusion. Through his clinical experiments and therapy, Freud concluded that the human mind was driven by a host of strong subconscious forces vying for power. We are governed by the unconscious and not by reason.

A follower of Darwin, Freud believed in an evolving world of chance events. Humans are essentially animals driven by instincts constantly in collision with societal standards. Belief in God is a neurosis, an illusion needed by the weak. Psychoanalysis, Freud thought, exposed religion for what it was—a psychological defense, not an actual reality. But not only was religion debunked, so was humanity. Freud once said, "Man is not a being different from animals or superior to them."[6] Humanity's unique feature is its confusion, dissatisfaction and anxiety; the animal kingdom has no need of psychotherapists.

Despite Freud's prolific genius—a genius that solidified a whole school of thought—a group of dissenters raised their voices, the most notable of which was Carl Jung (1875-1961). Jung, although an early disciple of Freud, questioned his mentor's reduction of all human behavior to sexual impulse. He likewise took exception to the notion that religious beliefs were nothing but harmful illusions. While Freud's view of the subconscious was that of a dark cauldron of powerful forces largely beyond our conscious control, Jung took a more positive view which left room for the mystical and religious (although in psychoanalytical redefined terms). Jung also posited a "collective unconscious"—a reservoir of psychological images and forces accruing through all history and shared by all people. Jung's approach makes him quite popular in New Age circles.

Wilhelm Reich (1897–1957) similarly left the Freudian orbit to develop the idea that blockages to personality development were recorded in muscular patterns in the body, forming what he called "character armor." Neurosis, he thought, had a physiological basis: the character armor hindered his patients from psychological recovery. Lifting the Freudian taboo against touching patients, Reich developed a form of bodywork to release the "orgone energy" that permeated the universe. Reich's ideas were essentially pantheistic and adventuresome. He designed "orgone accumulators" to collect and concentrate this mysterious cosmic energy. His theories went far beyond Freud and now play an important part in some New Age psychologies.

Despite Freud's popularity, a host of modern psychologists and critics have come to question many of Freud's assertions. Freudian theory, for all its imaginative ingenuity and sophistication, is little more than theory. His speculations concerning the dynamics of the subconscious are largely unprovable and questionable.[7]

The practice of psychoanalysis has also come under fire. O. Hobart Mowrer states that "today we can say, without fear of contradiction, that psychoanalysis has *not* been a 'success,' in this or any other country."[8] Martin Gross, after surveying the research, suggests that psychotherapy is overrated if not completely fallacious in its claims.[9]

Freud's reduction of religious belief to neurosis has been strongly and effectively challenged by another dissenting psychoanalyst, Viktor Frankl. Frankl's experience as a Jewish prisoner in Nazi Germany showed him that those prisoners with a will to live had a meaning for their lives beyond the random murder, torture and dehumanization of their immediate situation.[10] Those who had no outside hopes eventually died. Frankl believes that the central problem of modern man is "the existential vacuum," the loss of meaning. Whereas Freud actually went so far as to say that "the moment one inquires into the sense of value of life, one is sick," Frankl affirms that "the will to meaning" is crucial in human psychology.[11] Rather than dismiss human values as mere "reaction formations" or "defense mechanisms," Frankl sees them as irreducible components of the psyche. He says, "I am not prepared to live for the sake of my reaction formations, even less to die for the sake of my defense mechanisms."[12] The idea that a religious martyr died for nothing more than sublimated sexual urges is repellent to Frankl and many others.

## Skinner

While Freud demoralized humanity by reducing us to unconscious forces, another school of modern psychology explained human behavior exclusively according to external stimulation. With scientific rigor, behaviorism also saw humans as animals, but programmed animals. We are programmed not by our unconscious but by our environment; behavior consists of responses to stimuli.

Science, behaviorists claim, cannot study the mind, but must limit itself to behavior. B. F. Skinner systematized and propagated an all-encompassing behaviorism that denied humanity's free will and moral independence. Peace and harmony for humanity can only be attained through a completely controlled environment. Ordinary ideas of freedom and dignity are unscientific.

Skinner and other behaviorists have been criticized for basing most of their theories on the activities of rats and pigeons, rather than on the more complex dynamics of *human* behavior. Even the idea that animals are totally controlled by external stimuli has been seriously challenged by recent experiments in which pigs, racoons and chickens did not respond according to Skinner's theory of operant conditioning (the idea that all behavior can be controlled by positive or negative reinforcement).[13]

Without denying the fact that the environment shapes behavior, we can see that Skinner's conceptual box was too small to encompass human (or even animal) reality. Both scientific criticism and humanity's innate rejection of any theory that places us "beyond freedom and dignity" forced many to look beyond the dehumanizing confines of behaviorism for a broader and more human understanding of psychology. Just as many rejected the Freudian vision of humanity, behaviorism also proved fruitless. For Freud, human behavior was constrained by the inner necessities of the psyche; for Skinner, by the determinism of the environment. Both men were brilliant; yet the constraints their views imposed on human freedom proved intolerable.

## The Farther Reaches of Human Nature

Into this arid psychological landscape came the revolutionary ideas of Abraham Maslow (1908–1970), a man who saw another, almost forgotten side of humanity. In his landmark book *Motivation and Personality* (1954) Maslow elevated humanity above the animals, seeing people as essentially healthy beings capable of self-transcendence and great personal achievement. Rejecting Freudian and behavioristic reductionism, Maslow saw in people more potential than pathology. He said, "To oversimplify the matter somewhat, it is as if Freud supplied to us the sick half of psychology and we must now fill out the healthy half."[14] Maslow found a positive, "self-actualizing" force within each person that is struggling to assert itself. While Freud considered the inner nature hopelessly confused and Skinner considered it not at all, Maslow believed that since our "inner nature is good or neutral rather than bad, it is best to bring it out and encourage it rather than to suppress it. If it is permitted to guide our life, we grow healthy, fruitful, and happy."[15]

Maslow's research disclosed a "hierarchy of needs" ranging from the lower, biological ones to the higher, social needs. He claimed that our needs go beyond the material; we need to become self-actualized by satisfying our growth needs. Far more than simply satisfying sexual needs (Freud) or being socially conditioned (Skinner), a self-actualized person can experience "being-values" such as wholeness, perfection, completion, justice, aliveness, richness, simplicity, beauty, goodness, uniqueness, effortlessness, playfulness, truth and self-sufficiency.[16] These values can be realized in "peak experiences."[17] We are motivated by these higher needs and have within us the potential for their actualization.

In a passage reminiscent of Nietzsche's declaration that "man is something to be overcome," Maslow says that "transcendence also means to become divine or godlike, to go beyond the merely human." Yet Maslow denies that this implies the "supernatural" or "extrahuman" and so avoids any theological entanglement; his is an anthropological transcendence. He prefers the word *metahuman* or *B-human* (meaning Being Human) "in order to stress that his becoming very high or divine or godlike is part of human nature even though it is not often seen in fact." This is a "potentiality of human nature" and not a gift from God.[18]

Without leaving the naturalistic world view, Maslow smuggled in ultimate values, purpose and meaning. He did not deny many of the legitimate findings of psychoanalysis and behaviorism, but sought to move beyond them. Seeking to redignify a psychologically humiliated humanity, he bolstered the pummeled psyche with a liberal dose of optimism. Though an atheist himself, Maslow invested humanity with the attributes of deity. Such a realization, he thought, would be revolutionary. "It can and will change the world and everything in it," Maslow wrote in a personal letter. "I feel so privileged to be at a turning point in history."[19]

Maslow's pathbreaking efforts cleared the way for an exodus from the old psychological view of humanity toward a new human that is essentially good and has within himself unlimited potential for growth. A whole host of thinkers—Erich Fromm, Rollo May, Carl Rogers and others—sound this call. In humanistic psychology the self is seen as the radiant heart of health, and psychotherapy must strive to get the person in touch with that source of goodness. Thus Carl Rogers's method stresses a "client-centered" approach. The therapist is there to guide and catalyze, not to instruct or direct; the client has the answers within; they must simply be brought into the light. Human experience is thus the center and source of meaning and is valuable apart from any dependence on or subservience to a higher power.

This is the message at the core of New Age teaching. In Erich Fromm we see humanistic psychology being aligned with the experience of the One. Fromm views the biblical "myth" of the Fall as portraying "the first act of freedom." The act of disobeying God's commandment is our liberation from coercion and "the beginning of reason."[20] In describing humanistic religion, Fromm asserts that "God is a symbol of *man's own powers* which he tries to realize in his life, and is not a symbol of force and domination, having *power over man.*" For Fromm "virtue is self-realization, not obedience."[21] Part of this realization involves the One: "Religious experience in [humanistic] religion is the experience of oneness with the All, based on one's relatedness to the world as it is grasped with thought and with love."[22] Fromm also saw affinities between Zen Buddhism and Western psychoanalysis and agreed with the prolific Zen Buddhist writer D. T. Suzuki that the "Buddha nature is in all of us."[23] Fromm's testimony unites humanism and pantheism: the power is within, the One is waiting there. Fromm defines his position as "nontheistic mysticism"—the mysticism of humanity.

## The Human Potential Movement

From the germinal thoughts of humanistic psychology grew more developed perspectives, forming what is now called the human potential movement, a prime component of the New Age. Emerging in a time of insecurity and anxiety, by the 1970s the human potential movement spanned a number of therapies which Alvin Toffler described as "odds and ends of psychoanalysis, Eastern religion, sexual experimentation, game playing, and old-time revivalism."[24]

Ranging from the low-key pop-psychology of transactional analysis ("I'm O.K., You're O.K.") to the myriad of encounter groups begun by Carl Rogers, the movement stressed human goodness and potential. The Esalen Institute in Big Sur, California, has been a human potential "hothouse" for over three decades. Prominent at Esalen have been Michael Murphy and George Leonard, both pioneers of the New Age movement in America. Esalen has also sponsored Swami Muktananda and other assorted holy men, swamis, yogis and gurus. Calling it "the Harvard of the human potential movement," Jeffrey Klein notes that Esalen was responsible for exporting "virtually all the avant-garde psychological methods of the 1960s."[25] A recent Esalen catalog of events promises an experience where "your discoveries are your truth without needing outside validation."

This same spirit of autonomy and human potential animated the est movement and its derivative groups. Est (Erhard Seminar Training), Lifespring, Forum and other short seminars compact the One for all into intensive meetings where old beliefs are torn down and the supremacy of the self is proclaimed. Mixing together elements of Freudian theory, behavior-modification techniques, Eastern philosophy and humanistic psychology in a mass-marketable, mass-reproducible scale, est drilled its students with hard-core pantheism. We are, they say, "gods of our own universes" in complete control of all that happens to us.

## Transpersonal Psychology

But human potential thinking is not limited to popular seminars or strange therapies. A wholly new school of psychology is struggling to emerge as the dominant path to human understanding. This new school is called "transpersonal psychology" and is a logical extension of the humanistic school. Anthony Sutich in the first issue of the *Journal of Transpersonal Psychology* (Spring 1969), described trans-personal psychology (or "fourth force psychology") as an emerging force interested in "ultimate human capacities" not incorporated into behaviorism (first force), classical psychoanalysis (second force), or humanistic psychology (third force). Among those capacities listed are unitive consciousness, peak experiences, mystical experience, self-actualization, oneness, cosmic awareness, and transcendental phenomena.[26]

Agreeing with Maslow and others, transpersonal psychology rec-ognizes the need for transcendence in human experience. We must break free from reductionistic boxes. The "transpersonal" or spiritual dimension must be recovered and cultivated. One New Age book defines "transpersonal" as "referring to those dimensions of being or consciousness wherein individuals share a common identity; those dimensions wherein we are one."[27] Transpersonal theorists such as Ken Wilber, Charles Tart and others seek to integrate the New Age, "spiritual" understanding of humanity into the transpersonal, human potential perspective.

While transpersonal psychology has yet to become a dominant force in modern psychology, the stage is set for its propagation and application. Transpersonal ideas are made popular by psychologist Gerald Jampolsky in his popular book, *Love Is Letting Go of Fear.* John F. Kennedy University in Orinda, California, offers a masters degree in transpersonal psychology, as does the California Institute of Trans-personal Psychology in Menlo Park, California. Beverly Galyean's con-fluent education also takes a transpersonal approach, emphasizing the child's "higher" or transpersonal self. More sophisticated efforts are made by Ken Wilber whose transpersonal synthesis of the various schools of psychology makes his work intellectually appealing and places him on the cutting edge of the New Age intelligentsia.[28]

Transpersonal psychology embraces a variety of spiritual traditions (most prominently Eastern pantheistic and monistic religions) and encourages Eastern forms of meditation, yoga and various methods of consciousness expansion. In its synthesis of the humanistic position with spiritual disciplines, the movement offers both the credibility of Western thought and the exotic allurement of the East. Although it incorporates the ideas of Western sages, it also embraces the occult.[29]

The self, when divorced from a higher, transcendent power to whom it is accountable, quickly masquerades as the Self, a treasury of all meaning, power and wisdom. The old-fashioned secular humanist (including the orthodox Freudian or Skinnerian) said, "There is no Deity. Long live humanity." The new transpersonal or cosmic humanist says, "There is no Deity but humanity." God is pulled into the human breast. Scientific prowess and rationality as the crowning human achievements are outstripped by psychic abilities and unlimited potential.

## Self-Actualization and Morality
Much of the human potential movement assumes that self-actualization is an end in itself, irrespective of its effects on others. As we discover the One within, we act so as to release its potential in whatever way is most effective. The self knows best, apart from the traditional constraints of morality. As one observer put it, "Because personal experience equals reality, one changes reality by focusing on the self."[30] All events, people and things become instrumental in the actualization of self and become subservient to that goal. So, "concerns for self-sacrifice, sustaining relationships, and community responsibility inevitably erode."[31] The urge for transpersonal transcendence may take precedence over the tears, fears and pain of human relationships.

Carl Raschke labels this self-centered approach "subjectivism," which is "the stance of total disengagement from the meaning systems and value orientations of the communities in which one participates."[32] Raschke cites John Stevens's book, _Awareness,_ which says, "Full awareness of my experience requires complete acceptance of that experience as it is. Any demands—by myself or others—to be different than I am, reduces my contact with what I actually experience."[33]

Philosophically this is named "solipsism"; psychologically it may well be called "narcissism," the infatuation with self. Ironically, while New Age psychologies promise liberation from the individual limited self, they end by deifying a very isolated and autonomous self. One is imprisoned in one's own experience. Reality itself is lost when the universe is reduced to a "multiverse" of independently existing bubbles of subjective meaning. Believing in impossible things doesn't _ipso facto_ make them possible. In fact such "self-actualization" may result in far more alienations than actualizations, as the solipsist obliviously estranges those not in tune with his or her "space" (subjective reality). Raschke calls this collective solipsism "the atomization of experience," which "goes hand in hand with the fragmentation of social institutions and the retreat of alienated personalities into the false security of pure immediacy."[34]

That which proclaims pantheism (all is god, all is one) produces polytheism (many "self-actualizing" gods). The disregard for objective morality and reality is seen in Joel Latner's _The Gestalt Therapy Book:_ "Questions of goodness and morality . . . are superfluous. The issue is whether we shall realize our possibilities or deny them."[35] Hence the sixties credo "do your own thing" gains psychological reinforcement.

### The Limits of Goodness
A deeper presupposition must also be questioned, one that fuels the entire human potential and New Age enterprise, namely, the inherent goodness of the self. Human potential and transpersonal thought assume the unity of the self with the All, which conveys to the self power and authority. Oneness with the One is good for the self, and

the experience of the One leads to self-actualization. Evil is simply ignorance of one's true potential and a frustration of the natural drive toward self-actualization. Yet something hinders the ascent to glory As Leonard Geller points out, how can one discern what is the true good self and what is based on error? "Unless there are clear guidelines or criteria for distinguishing the 'call' or 'appeal' of the true self from that of impostors, self-deception would be an ever present danger, leading frequently to harmful and undesirable actions justified in the name of conscience and authenticity."[36]

Rather than providing such criteria, Rogers simply assumes the goodness and trustworthiness of the self as a sacrosanct island of value. Geller points out that "for Rogers, as for many theorists within the enlightenment tradition, the inherent wisdom and goodness of the self (or any part thereof) is a self-evident truth, almost a metaphysical first principle."[37] The revolt against the Freudian abyss and the Skinnerian machinery produced an equally unbalanced deification of the "real self" (however that is to be found).

Maslow's theories likewise suffer from an overestimation of the self. The origin of human problems, for Maslow, lies in the same self that is yearning for the development of its intrinsic potential. Differing from thinkers such as Fromm, Maslow sees evil not as the product of social factors, but more as a failure to actualize potential or the frustration occurring when the self begins to develop.[38] Yet as the need for self-actualization is met, many people "still suffer from higher-order dysfunctions that make growth impossible."[39] Maslow calls these "metapathologies." Included are such problems as anomie, alienation, boredom, apathy, resignation, cynicism, joylessness, meaninglessness.

But if Maslow is to tie these intruders to the self, he must somehow explain their stubborn existence. He says society itself cannot be blamed for deploying the psychological invaders. They issue from within. Thus, according to Geller, "the individual must bear full responsibility for pathological conditions underlying the higher-order dysfunctions. Evil is rooted in the self, not the environment."[40] Maslow says, "The culture is sun and food and water; it is not the seed."[41]

The impetus to actualize is inherent in who we are; yet the meta-pathologies reveal internal disharmony and strife within us. From whence does it come? Here Maslow has the same problem as Rogers. According to Geller, "Once [a person's] inner nature is in conflict with or divided against itself, it is impossible to determine from within human nature which of the conflicting elements or tendencies is healthy and which is pathological. Each is equally part of what we are."[42] A divided self is hardly the pure fount of self-actualization. If the self is not in harmony with itself, it is not the source of pure good and self-actualization. Maslow cannot have it both ways.

### Divine or Inflated?

Mounting evidence, both experiential and empirical, points to human weakness and need, rather than self-sufficiency. Maslow's entire concept of "self-actualization" as a unifying impetus for all human endeavor seems more ideological than empirical. Paul Vitz points out that Maslow's investigations of self-actualized persons did not even include a control group (a group used as a standard with which to compare the experimental group). We know nothing about the backgrounds of the people Maslow studied—neither their economic and social status nor information about their childhood. Vitz believes that Maslow's subjects were already exceptional people, "intelligent, educated, talented, and physically healthy" and that Maslow's extrapolation that all people have similar innate potential is unfounded.[43] Vitz also points out questionable research methods employed by Carl Rogers in advocating his ideas.[44] Maslow, Rogers and other self-actualizing optimists to the contrary, psychological research is turning up some unpleasant truth about human nature.

Psychologist David Myers marshals disturbing experimental evidence that darkens the gleam of the supposedly pristine self. Myers concludes that human problems are not rooted in a poor view of the self, but in an inflated self-concept. We are naturally egotistical and unrealistically so. Self-deception, not self-actualization, is the true state of affairs. It is not that we're good although we think we're bad (the human potential understanding), but that we think we're good when we're actually not so good. Myers gives "six streams of data" which "merge to form a powerful river of evidence," demonstrating "the pervasiveness of pride."[45]

Stream one shows that we are more likely to accept credit than to admit failure. Experimenters find that people in many situations take credit for success by attributing that success to their own ability and effort, while they explain failure as resulting from factors beyond their control. In games combining skill and chance, such as Scrabble, success is understood according to skill, but defeat according to chance (bad breaks, not bad playing).[46]

Stream two reveals our predilection to overestimate ourselves. Almost all people see themselves as better than average. Most American business people see themselves as more ethical than most; most community residents view themselves as less prejudiced than others; and most drivers assume that they are better-than-average drivers. When asked to rate themselves in "ability to get along with others," *zero* per cent of the 829,000 students who answered the poll thought themselves below average, sixty per cent saw themselves in the top ten per cent, and twenty-five per cent rated themselves in the top one per cent.[47]

Stream three uncovers our propensity to justify ourselves in spite of the facts. Not only do we take credit for what we may not be entitled to (stream one), we also deny responsibility for what we have done wrong. The most evil deeds are subsequently rationalized.[48]

Stream four Myers labels "cognitive conceit." We consistently overestimate our beliefs and judgments—whether in sports, politics or personal relations—so as to assume our own infallibility and prophetic eloquence.[49] This is seen in the "I knew it all along" phenomenon, in which people take credit for predicting an outcome of an event *after* it happens, thus vindicating their own insight.

Stream five concerns our unrealistic optimism, or what Myers calls "the Pollyanna syndrome." We "more readily perceive, remember and communicate pleasant [information] . . . than unpleasant information."[50] Myers notes that Weinstein's experiments with Rutgers University students discerned a tendency for most students to deem themselves more likely to succeed than their classmates in the areas of work, family and general happiness.

Stream six shows our tendency to overestimate how desirably we would act in certain situations. Researcher Steven Sherman called residents of Bloomington, Indiana, requesting they volunteer three hours to an American Cancer Society drive. Four per cent agreed. When he called a comparable group of residents and asked what they would do if called for such service, one half responded that they would help. We also remember compliments better than insults; and "we guess that physically attractive people have personalities more like our own than do unattractive people."[51]

Myers concludes by saying, "Unless we close our eyes to a whole river of evidence, it . . . seems that the most common error in people's self-images is not unrealistically low self-esteem, but rather a self-serving bias; not an inferiority complex, but a superiority complex."[52] Certainly if such "superiority complexes" were rooted in reality—if we all were innocent of failure, perfect in our self-estimation, never guilty of rationalization, true in our optimism and accurate in predicting our actions—we would have sure footing to climb the ladder of self-actualization with self-confidence and unfailing hope. Yet the ladder breaks and we fall, all the while rationalizing the descent according to our self-deception. Undoubtedly, not all people suffer from "the inflated self" in the same degree; some people do falsely condemn themselves because of various psychological reasons.[53] But who can honestly say, "I have kept my heart pure; I am clean and without sin" (Prov 20:9)? Can the mere lack of understanding of the self's supposed potential really account for humanity's long history of savagery and slaughter?

Erich Fromm argues in *The Anatomy of Human Destructiveness* that social evils are the result of bad societies, not bad people. But how do societies decay—whether it be Nazi Germany or modern America—if not because of people's attitudes, actions and beliefs? As Paul Vitz notes:

> Destructiveness, meanness, and hate are expressed daily in academic departments at universities and theological seminaries, government agencies, business organizations, assembly lines, and homes, in large cities and small towns. . . . Violent thoughts and fantasies and pet hatreds are some of our most familiar and pleasurable activities. We treasure them, even fondle them. History's great monsters are not really necessarily worse than you or I.[54]

As Paul Tournier has pointed out, the "violence is within." And all are guilty.

Yet despite humanity's self-deception, degeneracy and destructiveness there remains a "rumor of glory" (Bruce Cockburn), a hint of transcendence, a whiff of dignity and destiny. What is man, asked the psalmist, that God is mindful of him (Ps 8:4)?

## A Christian View of Human Nature

The biblical estimation of humanity need not deny the contribution of modern psychology, for in it Christianity finds corroboration for its ancient perspective. The enigma of man being simultaneously miserable and masterful is resolved by the Christian viewpoint. Blaise Pascal, the Christian philosopher and scientist, saw the need to meet the challenge.

> The greatness and wretchedness of man are so evident that the true religion must necessarily teach us both that there is in man some great source of greatness and a great source of wretchedness. It must then give us a reason for these astonishing contradictions.[55]

According to Christianity we are neither a chance collection of atoms nor a god. Here Christianity parts company with both secular humanism and New Age thinking. Humans have dignity and purpose because they are created in the image of their Creator (Gen 1:26). Yet unlike many other creation stories, Genesis does not declare or even suggest that we are emanations of God. We are creatures, creations of God brought into being by his creative will. Consequently, we resemble God analogously. A person is a "finite replica" of God. In this we see something of human greatness. New Age psychology in its many forms seeks to exalt humanity at the expense of human personality. Personality is often viewed as a hindrance to realization, something to be transcended once we enter the "transpersonal dimension." Yet biblically, being made in God's image involves being personal beings, as God is a personal being. This is a gift from God, not a curse. Human personality needs to be liberated from sin, not liquidated.

Like God, we have rationality and a sense of morality. Because God is the supreme and original Creator, we are also creative (although our creative activities merely use the materials and abilities given us by the Creator). We are also cultural beings who externalize our values and desires in social structures. We are foremost religious beings who seek to put our rationality, morality and creativity to service for some ultimate end. Ultimately, we will either serve ourselves or God.

Although we are godlike, we are not God. Our very finitude or creatureliness stands as a permanent testimony to our limitations. The inescapable facts of death, disease and suffering throw us back to our fragility and dependence. As creatures, we are contingent and dependent on a constellation of factors, many beyond our control. Though we banish such rude thoughts from our minds by affirming our human potential for self-realization, the realities find us out. Imitations of God, whether through self-actualization or other means, are worse than bad acting; they are futility itself. We should reflect on Chesterton's approach to such pretension:

So you are the Creator and Redeemer of the world: but what a small world it must be! What a little heaven you must inhabit, with angels no bigger than butterflies. How sad it must be to be God; and an inadequate God! Is there really no life fuller and no love more marvelous than yours; and is it really in your small and painful pity that all flesh must put its faith? How much happier you would be, how much more of you there would be, if the hammer of a higher God could smash your small cosmos, scattering the stars like spangles, and leave you in the open, free like other men to look up as well as down![56]

The psychic inflation of New Age thought calls for "the hammer of a higher God," the hammer of persistent reality. Yes we have greatness, even in our present state, even considering our aberrations and aspirations for the impossible, because we are made in the image of God. But we are like deposed kings, as Pascal put it. Rumors of a past greatness persist, gnawing unforgettably in a dim memory. Pascal describes this from God's perspective:

I created man holy, innocent, perfect. I filled him with light and intelligence. I communicated to him my glory and my wonders. The eye of man saw the majesty of God. He was not then in the darkness which blinds him, nor subject to mortality and the woes that affect him. But he has not been able to sustain so great a glory without falling into pride. He wanted to make himself his own centre and independent of my help. He withdrew himself from my rule; and, finding his happiness in himself, I abandoned him to himself.[57]

The first three chapters of Genesis speak of our original state before God. God had given Adam and Eve all that was needed for fulfillment and service. All he commanded was obedience; he prohibited eating from the tree of the knowledge of good and evil. That was all. Yet the serpent's temptation was, "You shall be as gods." That is, you shall take it all in your own hands to fashion your own destiny according to your own standards and by your own strength.

By falling to this temptation they proclaimed their own self-sufficiency and pride. By disobeying God, they announced their own deity. Rather than trusting in God and his goodness (already manifestly demonstrated to them), they trusted in themselves. The heart of their sin was denying their creaturehood and asserting their own supremacy. As Reinhold Niebuhr put it: "Sin is occasioned precisely by the fact that man refuses to admit his 'creatureliness' and to acknowledge himself as merely a member of the total unity of life. He pretends to be more than he is."[58] Augustine saw the temptation of pride as self-defeating, not self-liberating: "This then is the original evil: man regards himself as his own light, and turns away from that light which would make himself light if he would set his heart on it."[59]

The Fall was the first human declaration of autonomy from God, which has since been perennially repeated in human history. Myers sees a universal significance in the Genesis account:

The Genesis story . . . captures the saga of prideful self-assertion and its alienating effect upon our relationship with one another and with God. [It] suggests a universal history. Adam is the prototypical human, Everyman, the archetype of human experience.[60]

The result of humanity's disobedience was God's curse. People became alienated from themselves psychologically; from others sociologically, economically and politically; from our environment ecologically; and, ultimately, from God.

Sin is essentially idolatry—giving something other than God the status of God. Idols are best unmasked and then shattered. The idol of the New Age is consciousness itself; cosmic humanism seeks to tap the divine within, to merge with the One. Yet in it all we see what Freud correctly called "the will to death" (*thanatos*—see Prov 8:36); for man is not God, the creature is not the Creator. Only God can play God; all other attempts are the pretense of impostors.

The emphasis in New Age psychology is on self-actualization of innate human potential. Christianity emphasizes our innate inability to please a holy God because of selfishness at the root of our being, but it does stress the potential of God's grace to transform individuals into the image of Christ, to become "new creations." This indeed requires the "transpersonal" dimension—not in the sense of confusing deity with humanity—because God, the Supreme Person, transcends our limitations and offers us hope, through Christ, for positive psychological change in this life and perfection in the next.

# The New God of Science

5

A MAN FINDS HIS WAY TO THE SCIENCE SECTION OF HIS FAVORITE BOOKSTORE after browsing in the religion section. Having more than a passing interest in both science and religion, he notices a curious thing. Were the books misplaced? Some of the same titles from the religion section are in the science section. What sort of double-mindedness is this?

Puzzled, he begins to leaf through the books: quantum mechanics, holography, Einstein, Buddha, physics, mystics. Having first been perplexed, our friend is now interested. After another ten minutes of skimming, he is positively intrigued. After a few weeks of reading, he is captivated. His library expands, as does his consciousness. He finds that the One for all is the one for science.

Today religion and science have come together in a new way; instead of a stand-off, we see a new partnership, even a wedding. After centuries of warfare peace breaks out. Science grasps hands with the spiritual, and together they follow the same path.

No insurgent cultural movement can long ignore science. The counterculture spurned modern technology in favor of the natural and primitive. Science and technology, they said, had become scientism and a barren materialism. But since being thrown to the wind, science has returned like an unexpected boomerang—returning not to injure but to inspire. The social credibility granted to science is being employed to empower the One for all. Books such as Fritjof Capra's *The Tao of Physics* and Michael Talbot's *Mysticism and the New Physics* argue that new theories about the nature of the cosmos have opened the scientific community to some new ideas: the unity of all things, the nonexistence of an independent external world and the unity of opposites. In other words, science has been brought face to face with ancient mysticism. But what has so transformed a rationalistic scientism into mysticism?

### The Fall of Newton

Until the turn of this century physics stood on the unshakable foundation of Newtonian mechanics. Building on the work of Galileo, Descartes and others, Isaac Newton's view of the cosmos undergirded scientific thinking for two hundred years and helped make the technological confidence of the Industrial Revolution possible. Newton saw the world as the working of predictable mechanical laws set in the context of absolute space and time. His laws of motion and gravitation were used to unravel the logic of creation.

The clockwork universe was born. The atoms of matter dutifully obeyed the inexorable laws of nature. Modern science smoothly ran along the Newtonian track of common-sensical causation for some time—until its collision with the quantum.

Albert Einstein was a revolutionary. His theory of relativity rattled the Newtonian cage of space and time. Without going into detail, relativity ushered Newton's view of time and space out the scientific backdoor. Space and time were no longer viewed as distinct and absolute. They were "relative" to each other and in relation to the fixed speed of light. Furthermore, Einstein's famous equation, $E = mc^2$, stated that matter and energy were not strictly separable; rather, all mass has energy and may be translated into energy—atomic energy, as the world later discovered. In light of this seismic shock, science looked for new models of the universe, since Newton's clockwork model had crumbled all around them.

And the earth continued to move under the new science's trembling feet. On December 14, 1900, quantum theory was born, and Max Planck was the father. Planck addressed the German Physical Society with the idea that "matter absorbed heat energy and emitted light energy discontinuously" in unexpected lumps or spurts called "energy packets" or, as Einstein called them, "quanta."[1] Later they would be called "photons." They acted unpredictably, not smoothly and politely as in the old mechanical model. The subatomic world was not a mosaic of hard bits of matter. But just what were the quanta? While Planck's formula helped explain the behavior of light, it created as many puzzles as it solved.

Planck's initial investigations of the quanta's flagrant disregard for mechanical etiquette propelled an international group of physicists in the first three decades of the century to attempt to formulate an adequate understanding of this strange subatomic realm. Men like Einstein, de Broglie, Schrödinger, Pauli, Dirac, Bohr and Heisenberg wrestled with enigmas at the heart of matter that would forever alter our understanding of the universe.

Experiments showed that light, always considered to be made of waves, sometimes acted like particles. These particles of light are the same photons that surprised Planck. They are not both a wave and a particle; they are actually neither a wave nor a particle. Instead they exhibit particlelike and wavelike functions.

The Danish physicist Niels Bohr accounted for this paradox by his *complementarity principle*. Bohr held that both the wave and particle explanations of light in fact described the same reality, each being appropriate in different ways. In other words, we have no common-sense model for how light works; we can't picture it. As philosopher of science Paul Davies puts it, "There is no everyday counterpart of a 'wave-particle,' so the microworld is not merely a Lilliputian version of the macroworld, it is something qualitatively different—almost paradoxically so."[2] But we must face it nonetheless.

But what are these strange subatomic critters and how can they be corralled? At most we can know only the probability of the where-abouts of these wave-particles. Werner Heisenberg's *uncertainty principle,* based on his study of the electron, helps us understand the problem. Unlike the world of larger sensible objects, the quantum world is not easily identified and mapped out. Heisenberg discovered that it is experimentally impossible to chart an electron's velocity and position simultaneously. When we measure the velocity, we exclude knowledge of position, and vice versa. Thus we cannot know the electron's future state; it is uncertain. In fact, the very act of meas-uring the electron influences its position. Heinz Pagels likens this to trying to determine the location and velocity of a tomato seed. If you try to measure the location by touching the seed, it will slip away. Measuring the position makes it change position. A similar slipper-iness is seen in Heisenberg's uncertainty principle.[3] Thus the strict separation between observer and observed is broken down.

These and other ideas have shaken the once solid world of New-tonian science such that Paul Davies subtitled his book on the new physics "a portrait of nature in rebellion." The old boxes could not contain it. Niels Bohr has said that "anyone who is not shocked by quantum theory has not understood it."[4] The world of mechanical certainties and precise calculation is behind us. Many such as Bohr and Heisenberg have even said that reality is at best run by chance (much to the consternation of Einstein, who said that God does not play dice with the universe). Yet the quantum theory which accounts for the behavior of scores of subatomic particles—which we cannot elaborate on here—has established itself among scientists as the best explanation of the events encountered. Pagels calls it "the most powerful mathematical tool for the explication of natural phenomena that ever fell into human hands, an incomparable achievement in the history of science."[5]

But to many the achievement is not limited to science; it is also a spiritual achievement, a marriage of science and religion. But how is this understood?

## The Quanta and the Buddha

The old conception of hard, mechanical matter is in disrepute. Matter is not reducible to neat, divisible pieces that mathematically obey the rules. According to Capra,

> Subatomic particles . . . are not "things" but are interconnections between "things," and these "things," in turn, are interconnections between other "things," and so on. In quantum theory you never end up with "things"; you always deal with interconnections.[6]

Capra believes that because we cannot cut up the universe into "independently existing smaller units," we must see its "basic oneness."[7] Theoretical physicist David Bohm speaks of an "implicate" or "unfolded" order of "unbroken wholeness" that binds all things together in unceasing fluctuation.[8] We must move from a fragmented viewpoint to one that encompasses the whole. Relativity and quantum theory, he believes, "imply the need to look on the world as an undivided whole, in which all parts of the universe, including the observer and his instruments, merge and unite in one totality."[9]

But according to Capra this is what the Eastern mystics have been saying for thousands of years: all is one. In Capra's very popular and influential book *The Tao of Physics* he finds parallels between the new physics and the mystics. By setting statements by physicists next to those of Buddhist, Taoist and Hindu mystics and Scriptures, he finds mutually supportive testimony for the oneness of all things, the unity of opposites (complementarity), the relativity of space and time, and the ever-changing nature of reality.[10] The old materialism gives ground to the Tao. In surveying a variety of theories "at the frontiers of science," Marilyn Ferguson says that "science is only now verifying what humankind has known intuitively since the dawn of history."[11]

## A World of Your Own

Heisenberg's uncertainty principle asserted that when observing, we affect what is observed. There is no strict subject-object split or dualism. We do not simply observe the universe, we participate in it. Capra says that "in Eastern mysticism [the] universal interwovenness always includes the human observer and his or her consciousness, and this is also true in atomic physics."[12]

Some have interpreted the uncertainty principle to mean that subatomic particles do not have an independent, external and objective existence. Their attributes (of being a wave or a particle) are dependent on their observation. Capra says, "The electron does not *have* objective properties independent of my mind."[13] In discussing Schrödinger's understanding of the quantum realm, Fred Alan Wolf comments that "the position of wholeness taken by Schrödinger I call *quantum solipsism.* According to solipsism, the self is the only thing that can be known and verified. . . . Everything depends on you. You create the whole universe; you are the 'you-niverse.' "[14]

Consciousness is thrust into the metaphysical driver's seat. Rather than recording reality, we determine it. This notion is fueled by another scientific breakthrough, the holographic paradigm. The hologram, discovered through photographic experiments, is a three-dimensional projection resulting from the interaction of laser beams. Unexpectedly, researchers found that the entire hologram could be reproduced from any one of its component parts. "Each part of the hologram, no matter how small, can reproduce the whole image when illuminated by laser light."[15]

This leads George Leonard to compare the hologram "to the Hindu idea of the Net of Jewels, in which every jewel, every piece of the universe, contains every other piece."[16] This, he believes, is the core of all mysticism: the "idea of all-in-oneness."[17] The Stanford neuroscientist Karl Pribram has proposed that the brain functions holographically because its abilities do not seem to be specifically located in various parts of the brain. This would explain how the destruction of certain parts of the brain do not always destroy a specific function.[18]

Without going into detail, the upshot for many New Age thinkers is that all knowledge is potentially contained in consciousness. Pribram has speculated that "maybe the *world* is a hologram!"[19] Leonard speculates that "in such a universe, information about the whole is available at its every point."[20] According to Michael Talbot, "the new physics suggests that the consciousness contains a 'reality structurer,' some neurophysiological mechanism which psychically affects reality itself."[21]

## Beyond the Ordinary

If consciousness "creates reality" and the whole is holographically contained in the parts, the prerogatives of the godhead are within us. The paranormal becomes possible, because all have equal access to the holographic domain. Ferguson suggests:

> In this framework, psychic phenomena are only by-products of the simultaneous-everywhere matrix. Individual brains are bits of the greater hologram. They have access under certain circumstances to all the information in the total cybernetic system.[22]

She further proposes that the holograph may provide the scientific model to explain the paranormal or psychic realm.

Paranormal manifestations, referred to as psi or, more traditionally, as extrasensory perception (ESP), have increasingly engaged the scientific community. J. B. Rhine's early work at Duke University has been augmented by a host of psychic researchers vying to gain scientific respectability. A large measure of respectability was granted to parapsychology in 1969 when the prestigious American Association for the Advancement of Science made the Parapsychological Association a member organization.[23]

The *Brain/Mind Bulletin,* edited by Marilyn Ferguson, announced that the University of Edinburgh, Scotland, has agreed to create a chair of parapsychology at the behest of the late Arthur Koestler. This is the first chair of its kind in a British university.[24] Numerous experiments have sought scientifically to validate parapsychological occurrences and have provoked opposition from dedicated critics, such as Martin Gardener, who dispute their scientific integrity.[25]

Despite the controversy, the paranormal has become a passion for millions, even for national governments. Both the Soviet Union and the United States government have funded parapsychological research relating to military intelligence and espionage. Parapsychological research has been supported by the United States government at SRI International (formerly, Stanford Research Institute) in Menlo Park, California, for over ten years.[26] Some claim that psychic research may receive as much as six million dollars annually from the Defense Department.[27]

Evidence gained from cultural exchange programs indicates that steps are also being taken in post-Maoist China to subsidize government research on psi phenomena, which they call Extraordinary Human Body Functions (EHBF). These include telepathy, clairvoyance and psychokinesis. These studies fit nicely into the traditional Chinese world view which identifies a universal life energy (ch'i) that connects all things.[28]

## The Tao of Physics or the Christ of Physics?
On the surface, the explosion of literature on the scientific evidence for the One is impressive: the old classical world view is in ruins; matter and energy meet and merge; quantum theory shows the interconnection of all things; the paranormal becomes normal and possible because all is interconnected and unified in the holographic paradigm.

But when we look beneath the surface, we find that the package is not as neatly wrapped as we had thought. One of the problems is that many of the New Age science writers, such as Capra, Talbot and Zukav, sometimes present controversial and contested scientific theories as though they were scientific facts. A noteworthy example concerns the interpretation of Heisenberg's uncertainty principle and the influence of the observer on the quantum realm. Many New Age writers assume that consciousness itself affects the quantum realm or even that reality springs into existence through the act of thinking. Yet this is contested by many physicists. A distinction must be made between the influence of the apparatus of observation and the influence of the consciousness of the observer. Ian Barbour clarifies this:

> The "involvement of the observer" refers to *observation processes* and not to mental states as such. The "frame of reference" means the measuring apparatus—clocks, meter sticks, photographic plates—not minds or persons. . . . It is the detection apparatus, not the observer as a human being, which influences the measurement obtained.[29]

In criticizing Gary Zukav's popular book *The Dancing Wu Li Masters* (which also finds parallels between science and Eastern mysticism), Robert John Russell noted that "one does not find a distinction made between experimental results and the interpretations based on them." Russell cites as an example Zukav's agreement with Eugene Wigner and John Von Neuman on the "central role of consciousness on elementary physical phenomena,' a disputed interpretation not held by many physicists.[30]

## Physics and Metaphysics

The conflict of theories drives us to deeper questions: what can science really tell us about reality? Can it tell us anything about God? The road from physics (scientific study of the creation) to metaphysics (the nature of all reality) is not as easily traveled as many New Age writers believe. There are several reasons for this.

First, *scientific theories are often short-lived.* The hallmark of to-day's science may be a tombstone tomorrow. Christian philosopher Gordon Clark states that

so rapid and so extensive have been the changes in physics since the abolition of ether and the invention of wavicles that one may confidently affirm that, whereas Newtonianism lasted for two centuries, no theory today seems likely to last two decades.[31]

Established theories often and easily become disestablished or substantially revised. Although Marilyn Ferguson harnesses a number of theories at "the frontiers of science" to pull us into the New Age, we must realize that the "frontiers" we arrive at may be tomorrow's wastelands.

Clark has also astutely commented that "scientific procedure does not invariably grasp the truth; on the contrary it has a long record of accepting what is later thought to be false."[32] Although a New Age theorist himself, Ken Wilber spots the problem of wedding mysticism to science: "To paraphrase Eckhart, if your god is the god of today's physics, then when the physics goes (tomorrow), that god will go with it."[33]

Second, *even within any one period of time, scientists disagree on the interpretation of any scientific theory.* While quantum mechanics now commands the day, scientists differ on just how it should be interpreted. Some, like Wigner and Schrödinger, see it as demanding solipsism (all is mind); others, as mentioned above, are unconvinced. Some, like Bohr and Heisenberg, see it as revealing a chance universe; others, like Einstein and Bohm, do not. Ken Wilber also sees the dangers of uncritically wedding disputed theories with the New Consciousness: "To hook transpersonal psychology/mysticism to the consensus of the new quantum mechanics is not possible, because there is no consensus. Those connections that have been drawn between physics and mysticism are of the pick and choose variety."[34] The scientific jury is always out—if not hung.

Third, *such disagreement among scientists indicates that scientific*

*theorizing and speculating is not purely and simply an objective mat-
ter of empirical observation.* The world view of the scientist necessarily affects their view of their studies. This is unavoidable. Capra
admits to his bias after summarizing the new physics in *The Turning
Point:*

> My presentation of modern physics . . . has been influenced by my
> personal beliefs and allegiances. I have emphasized certain con-
> cepts and theories that are not yet accepted by the majority of
> physicists, but that I consider significant philosophically, of great
> importance for the other sciences and for our culture as a whole.[35]

In his earlier book, *The Tao of Physics,* he began by reporting a
profound mystical experience that affected his later integration of
physics and mysticism.[36]

Christian philosopher Arthur Holmes makes the point that a value-
free or absolutely objective science is impossible because "science
itself is a human enterprise dependent on beliefs and values—even
on the world views—that scientists themselves bring to science rather than simply drawing them from their work."[37] Furthermore, Thomas Kuhn, in his influential work *The Structure of Scientific Revolutions,* has argued that revolutions in scientific theories (which he calls
"paradigm shifts") often result from psychological and sociological
influence more than from empirical and logical factors. This is not to
opt for total skepticism but rather to consider carefully the scientific
claims in their overall context.

Fourth, *the appeal to even the most well-established scientific theory for a metaphysical system is problematic because of the inherent
limitations of the scientific method itself.* If we define science as the
"empirical and theoretical inquiry into natural processes and relationships,"[38] it is barred from making comprehensive and indisputa-
ble pronouncements about ultimate reality. Science informs a world
view but cannot, by itself, create one. As Holmes says, "to extrapolate
from *what is empirically observable to everything that is* involves a
logical *non sequitur.*"[39] In a book debunking some of the pretenses

of modern science, Anthony Standen notes that "physics is a splendid subject, as far as it goes, but it doesn't go far enough. It doesn't go any further than just physics—the physical world."[40]

Scientific induction, for that matter, has difficulty establishing an absolute, for any new discovery could conceivably overthrow all previous speculations. Standen notes that "physics can never *prove* things in the way things are proved in mathematics, by eliminating *all* of the alternative possibilities. It is not possible to say what the alternative possibilities are."[41] Historian of science Stanley Jaki comments that "science keeps developing because there is no strict identity between any actual form of science and the full intelligibility of nature."[42] In other words, the state of science at any given time does not perfectly correspond with the state of objective reality. Even if quantum theory or other theories at "the frontiers of science" could demonstrate the substantial interconnection of all things, this would say nothing about God, who is above his created order.

Unfortunately, scientific conclusions (if we could call them that) are often seen as having implications outside of their proper domain. The philosopher of science Karl Popper called this "the law of unintended consequence." This was evident in the use of Einstein's theory of relativity to justify moral relativism. The theory concerned our understanding of space and time, not morality. It did not apply to ethics, a point about which Einstein himself was vehement. Nevertheless, relativity was confused with relativism.[43] Martin Gardener shows the irony of this mistake: "Relativity theory introduced all sorts of new absolutes. . . . Einstein originally considered calling relativity 'invariant theory'!"[44]

Similarly, the new physics is metaphysically taxed for more than it is worth. In reflecting on physical theories, Itzhak Bentov surmises that "there is a level of Nature at which all extremes become reconciled and merged. It is on this level that black and white, good and evil merge into one 'Is'-ness." Bentov sees this as "the ultimate truth."[45] Talbot states that "in the new cosmology, we should learn to accept all cosmic eggs [world views] as correct, especially the ones we have chosen for ourselves."[46] While all these assertions are demanded by the One for all, they are not necessitated by the new physics.

## A Christian View of Creation and Science

The force of this criticism should drive us to realize that the scientific vindication of the One for all is unconvincing. In fact, the holographic paradigm's idea that we arbitrarily create reality through our acts of consciousness knocks the wind out of the scientific enterprise entirely. Not only is the solipsistic interpretation of quantum physics hotly debated among scientists, it is a philosophical land mine for the scientific method. If there is no objective, external reality independent of the observer in some substantial way, how can scientists compare their findings with each other? To test hypotheses meaningfully, a shared field of experience is necessary. Put simply, scientists must be talking about the same thing, despite whatever subjective factors influence them. Richard Bube, a scientist and Christian, comments:

> Authentic science is unreservedly committed to the existence of an objective reality. . . . We need not suppose that this reality is static or even unchanging with time. . . . Nor need we suppose that this reality is unaffected by us or our perceptions of it. . . . To speak of an objective reality in the sense here used is to affirm that the character of things exists outside the self or the individual human being; it is what it is and does not depend on me.[47]

Bube criticizes the New Age idea that we construct reality instead of discover it: "Such a position, if carried to its rational conclusion, involves a radical break with all traditional understanding of authentic science and opens the door to a subjective existentialism in which terms like truth, reality, and objectivity become mere symbols without content."[48] But the terms *truth, reality* and *objectivity* do have content in a Christian view of the world and science.

Many scholars have documented the connection between the Christian world view of the modern West and the development of modern science. Scientists such as Galileo, Kepler and Newton presupposed that the universe was created by a rational God and was itself rationally constructed. They therefore pursued science with the faith that the creation could be explored through rational discovery. God, they believed, fitted our rationality for understanding the objective world. Jaki cites evidence showing that without this theistic world view science falters: "Science found its only viable birth within a cultural matrix permeated by a firm conviction about the mind's ability to find in the realm of things and persons a pointer to their Creator."[49]

Yet Christianity need not endorse the mechanistic cosmology that emerged from prequantum science. While biblical faith affirms God's governance over and in all things, it need not reduce the workings of all of creation to a mechanistic model. Capra and other New Age critics often confuse the biblical model of creation with a deistic view—God turned on the machine, but it runs by itself. But the God of the Bible is not a deistic clockmaker totally removed from creation; neither is creation fully comprehended by a narrow rationalism. Rather the universe is created and unified by Christ, the Logos or Word of God (Jn 1:1-14), who personally directs and coordinates the richness of the cosmic drama without pantheistically merging with it (Col 1:15-20; Heb 1:3). The Dutch theologian Abraham Kuyper stresses this point by saying, "There is on earth no life, energy, law, atom, or element but the Almighty and Omnipresent God [who] quickens and supports that life from moment to moment, causes that energy to work, and enforces that law."[50]

Rather than animating the cosmos with a pantheistic consciousness of its own, biblical faith knows the unity and harmony of the creation to be the product of God's governance. The mechanistic model is appropriate in certain spheres, but not all; if made absolute it suffers from a conceptual squint that becomes blind to the larger picture and mystery. Instead of throwing us into the eager arms of the One for all, the enigmas of modern science should fill us with awe and wonder as we tremble before the creative immensities of God— immensities that rudely remind us of our inescapable finitude in struggling to understand God's creation. We can understand and explore God's creation, but we cannot completely comprehend it. We cannot bottle up and dole out the mysteries of God's providence. Finite minds, though enlightened by the Logos (Jn 1:9), are barred from the infinite understanding required to untie every scientific knot (or chart every subatomic particle).

A biblical cosmology is not offended by modern speculations on the unity and interconnection of creation. While we must view such scientific theories with caution, the Bible pictures a God who sustains and unifies creation without violating the created integrity of distinct entities. (God created and sustains each according to its kind—Gen 1:11-25.) Rather than a monistic cosmology, the biblical view of creation harmonizes the one (unity of creation) with the many (distinct creations). The biblical view, then, is holistic without being monistic. Pascal, the Christian philosopher and scientist, realized this long ago when he said that "all is held together by a natural though imperceptible chain which binds together things most distant and different; [therefore] I hold it equally impossible to know the parts without knowing the whole and to know the whole without knowing the parts in detail."[51]

The biblical view affirms both the transcendence and immanence of God and so establishes the importance and integrity of the creation. Far from demeaning or exploiting the creation, biblical faith entails an ecological theology as the many Old Testament laws relating to the land demonstrate.[52] Once extracted from its pantheistic elements, *general systems theory* (which combines physics, biology and other sciences in a unified view of the world and is espoused by Capra and others) may be serviceable for Christian cosmology in helping to provide a model for how the processes of providence work.[53]

## New Age Science in Question

New Age science ends up bowing to the mysteries of creation instead of worshiping the Creator. It views the interconnected web of existence as the final reality, instead of seeing it as a pointer to God. In its misguided worship it renders its god as an impersonal consciousness or force instead of the personal Creator and Lord over all. This demotion of the Deity proves problematic for the New Age cosmology, for its deity must do metaphysical double duty: the One must unify and embody the cosmos, *and* it must also provide purpose, stability and meaning for personal beings (we humans). Yet it is *impersonal*—"neither male nor female, nor manifest in any personal form."[54] In contrast to the infinite and personal God of the Bible, such a deity hardly seems up for the task.

Because of the limitations of science previously discussed, parapsychology has yet to receive scientific vindication. Experiences and experiments supposedly demonstrating the paranormal are often open to rational questioning. Psychologist David Myers points out our natural credulity and desire to witness the supernatural despite insufficient evidence. The skills of the trained magician may trick us into interpreting sleight of hand as a paranormal event. This is heightened in an age that feels the futility of a godless universe and yearns for comfort and intrigue from a supernatural realm. Myers speaks of the pride that is "evident in the yearning for God-like omniscience—reading other people's minds, and foretelling the future."[55]

In its intoxication with creation—which it mistakes for the One—the New Age tends to ignore the ever-present reality of sin and the Fall. With its interest in the paranormal and parapsychology, it opens a Pandora's box of potential poisons. While it is true that much of what purports to be paranormal is either trickery or misinterpreted phenomena, the Christian world view affirms the existence of supernatural entities (both good and evil) who can and do influence the natural realm. Paranormal demonic activity may appear to many as evidence for humankind's inherent paranormal potential.

If the paranormal world is courted without the protection and guidance of Christ, what began as romance may end as psychic violence. This was the case with the Jewish exorcists recorded in the book of Acts. Attempting to cast out a demon by their own strength, they were beaten and bloodied by the uncooperative spirit (Acts 19:13–16). Despite the scientific respectability sometimes given to the paranormal, apart from the lordship of Christ it is nothing other than the occultism prohibited throughout the Bible. It is the search for power in the wrong place. The shaman returns in scientific guise, still toting his bag of spiritual poison. James Sire clearly sees the problem:

> The new consciousness has reopened a door closed since Christianity drove the demons from the woods, desacralized the natural world and generally took a dim view of excessive interest in the affairs of Satan's kingdom of fallen angels. Now they are back, knocking on university dorm doors, sneaking around psychology laboratories and chilling the spines of ouija players. Modern man has fled from his grandfather's clockwork universe to his great-great grandfather's chamber of gothic horrors![56]

Both those who falsely think they have experienced the paranormal (when they have instead misinterpreted a natural event) and those who have trafficked in occult energies are under the illusion of pantheistic self-sufficiency—that they possess and control the paranormal within them, that they have infinite potential. Theodore Roszak muses that " 'impossibilities' may only be realities vibrating in a wavelength of the mind we—or most of us—have not yet learned to tune in. Perhaps nothing we have ever imagined is beyond our powers."[57]

Another prophet, one familiar with a culture enticed by spiritual counterfeits, preached another message. Jeremiah said, "Cursed is the one who trusts in man, who depends on flesh for his strength and whose heart turns away from the LORD. . . . But blessed is the man who trusts in the LORD, whose confidence is in him" (Jer 17:5, 7).[58]

# The Politics of
# Transformation

## 6

WHAT BEGINS IN MYSTICISM ENDS IN POLITICS, A FRENCH POET ONCE SAID.
William Irwin Thompson has observed that in our day "it is the mystic
who has become the unacknowledged legislator of the world."[1] Both
comments spotlight the truth that religion can never be severed from
politics. Political vision stems from our deepest beliefs concerning
reality and value. Politics follows faith.

It is not surprising, then, that the New Age has a political agenda
or that the One is being taken to the streets, into political caucuses,
before the halls of civil government and into the ballot box. Having
penetrated the fields of psychology, science and medicine, the New
Age is seeking to enter and capture the world of politics. The whole
society must be brought into harmony with the One as the New
Consciousness produces the New Age.

New Age politics—sometimes called transformationalist politics—

attempts to cut to the root of our political disease. Marilyn Ferguson says "the political system needs to be *transformed,* not *reformed.*"[2] This transformation requires not merely a change of political structure but a new consciousness. This brand of politics must step into the gap by transcending traditional ideologies and our present political purposelessness. In fact, it calls for a whole new world view.

## Spiritualizing the Left

Much of the upheaval of the 1960s counterculture was political. Demonstrations, sit-ins, riots and general rebellion against "the establishment" characterized the hippie culture. The social and political conservatism of the 1950s was challenged by a new political radicalism discontent with old answers. The crisis and embarrassment of the Vietnam War chafed at the sensibilities of the idealistic youth culture. A radical and often Neo-Marxist left emerged to challenge both the Vietnam involvement and Nixon's political conservatism in general. Led by the social philosophy of Herbert Marcuse and others, scores of college students rallied against what they saw as the decadence of American politics. More anarchistic rebels such as Abbie Hoffman and Jerry Rubin engaged in outrageous antics to foment "the revolution" to bring down the status quo.

But after the shooting of several protesting students by the National Guard at Kent State University, the political nerve of the radical left began to fail. With the end of American involvement in Vietnam, stability returned to the once turbulent college campuses and the old radicalism lost the energy generated by a common enemy—the war.

The seventies saw many activists turn inward to find solutions not found through militant politics. The war in Vietnam may have ended but the psychological struggle for peace and wholeness was far from over for many in the counterculture. Jerry Rubin describes this sojourn from political activism to spiritual discovery in his book *Growing (Up) at Thirty-Seven.* His spiritual aspirations led him into est, yoga and other human potential therapies and practices. Like Rubin, many turned inward in the seventies after the outward political outrage of the sixties.

Yet Rubin did not stay in a cocoon of subjectivity; instead he re-emerged with an expanded vision of social transformation. Now with a spiritually recharged exuberance, Rubin proclaims that "as the consciousness movement expands, its natural evolution will be toward changing society, taking the new energy generated through meditation, yoga, honesty, and self awareness outward into social institutions."[3] In 1976, Rubin complained that "the consciousness movement" was not yet politically engaged, but that it had the potential to powerfully "unite spirituality and politics" and to create "the total human being on a mass scale, as we develop ourselves in all aspects of our being."[4] Now in the eighties his hope has become prophetic as "the Aquarian Conspiracy" has begun to put the New Age on the political map.

For many, the countercultural protest has developed into the New Age hope for the total transformation of self and society. While many liberal political elements remain, the leftism of the sixties has been transcended by a spiritual politics not content with secular materialism. Mark Satin claims that we are more than simply economic beings, and our liberation must include a spiritual as well as an economic recovery.[5] In short, the New Age political message is: our consciousness is unlimited and our responsibility is total. As gods come of age we must transform the planet.

## Crisis and Transformation

Although New Age politics has yet to substantially influence the political climate, various social and political conditions may give it a chance. First, the growing influence and popularity of pantheism in psychology, science, health care and religious practices are bound to spill over into the political arena. As said earlier, what begins in mysticism ends in politics. If the One can displace secular materialism in one realm after another, it will not stop short of the state.

Second, many in the post-Watergate culture are disillusioned with traditional political answers. Recent voter apathy and the growing popularity of nontraditional political parties, such as the Citizen's Party and the Libertarians, demonstrate a thirst for something new. Further, the severity of the world situation cries out for a renewed political vision. The arms race, world hunger, ecological disturbances and economic distress breathe heavily down the neck of the established political order. More and more people feel something radical must be done.

Third, many view our age of crisis as a time of unparalleled potential for transformation. A new age opens before us. Alvin Toffler, whose tremendously successful *Future Shock* sparked widespread general interest in rapid social change, sees civilization swept over by a "third wave." We face the dawn of a new civilization which is "the single most explosive fact of our lifetime."[6] For Toffler, this new civilization will introduce different family lifestyles, changed ways of work, a new economy and politics, and "beyond all this an altered consciousness as well."[7] The stakes are high and the challenge monumental, but we face "a quantum leap forward."[8]

Fourth, New Age politics combines an otherwise diverse group of social movements in the hope of presenting a unified alternative to what Satin calls the American political "prison."[9] He sees "the new politics" arising from "the feminist, environmental, spiritual, and human potential movements; the appropriate technology, simple living, decentralist, and 'world order' movements; the business-for-learning-and-pleasure movement and the humanistic-transformational education movement."[10] Capra believes that once these movements "have recognized their common aims, [they] will flow together and form a powerful force of social transformation," which he calls "the rising culture."[11]

**The New Age Political Agenda**
The root idea of the New Age is oneness, unity and wholeness—the

One for all. The controlling metaphor for the "old paradigm" was the machine. The earth, the state and humanity were seen as assemblages of individual parts (atoms, as it were) isolated and insulated from each other. New Age politics seeks to replace this atomism with a holism that sees the planet as an interrelated system—an organism rather than a machine. The old narrowness of vision must succumb to a planetary consciousness, a global understanding of political reality.

This unified view leads to several distinctives. First, ecological issues of conservation and pollution control become crucial concerns in the political agenda. We must identify ourselves with nature and find our interrelation with all of life. Exploitative technologies and political policies must be replaced by an ecological perspective. Capra argues that we must enter the solar age and put aside dependence on fossil fuels.[12] Satin outlines several political strategies to help foster the transition from nuclear power and nonrenewable forms of energy to other forms.

Second, the traditional polarities between masculine and feminine must be transcended. Patriarchy must be replaced with an awareness of male-female equality or even, in some cases, of female superiority (as in some of the neo-pagan movement). Capra believes that one major modern crisis is the shift from patriarchy to a more balanced viewpoint that combines both the *yin* (feminine) and the *yang* (masculine), elements described in traditional Taoism.[13] Western culture has accented the yang while repressing the yin. This has led to an exploitative and rationalistic culture and political order. Charlene Spretnak, editor of *The Politics of Women's Spirituality,* believes that "the experiences inherent in women's sexuality are expressions of the essential, holistic nature of life on earth; they are 'body parables' of the profound oneness and interconnectedness of all matter/energy."[14] This awareness will lead to new political understanding and action.

Spretnak also believes that a sense of interconnection with the entire universe will stop us from violating others by "forcing them to give birth."[15] She thus uses pantheistic monism to justify abortion. Because of this and the New Age emphasis on moral relativism, its political agenda generally supports abortion on demand (as does the German Green Party).

Other issues such as population control and nuclear disarmament could be added, and it can be safely said that the heart of New Age politics beats with a liberal political pulse—although activists such as Satin speak of transcending the polarities of the political right and left.[16] But rather than narrowly focusing on single issues, there is a much broader theme we need to address: the goal of instituting a new world order.

## World Order

Cosmic consciousness knows all as one; New Age political consciousness knows the world as one also—one interlocking, interrelated, interpenetrating system. Therefore, the idea of strict national boundaries and divisions between nations and peoples must be transcended by the realization of unity and interdependence.

According to New Age activists, we all share a cosmic commonality that must be translated into political reality. Patriotism and nationalism result from the false consciousness of separation and exclusiveness.

Moreover, modern transportation and communication has, at least technologically, already unified the world. While no one within the movement can take credit for this international development, nonetheless many view it as a harbinger of the New Age. Nations and peoples once culturally and geographically isolated from each other are now brought face to face. As Mark Satin remarks, "Planetary events are, in a sense, *conspiring to inspire* us to recognize our oneness and interdependence."[17] The New Age sees this as the emergence of a global civilization, or, as Lewis Mumford put it, "a world culture." As early as 1956, Mumford wrote:

The destiny of mankind, after its long preparatory period of separation and differentiation, is at last to become one. . . . This unity is on the point of being politically expressed in a world government that will unite nations and regions in transactions beyond their individual capacity.[18]

Thompson speaks of this transition as moving from civilization to *planetization*.[19]

New Age politics, then, emphasizes the need for a political order consonant with the cosmic order. While most speak of the need for cultural uniqueness, New Age political thinkers point toward a new world order where the nations are united politically and economically. Since the enjoyment of wealth, prosperity and peace is now unevenly distributed, a new economic order is required to redress the balance. Likewise, strategies of nuclear disarmament must be implemented if the new global society is to live as one and in peace.

Satin speaks vaguely of a "planetary guidance system" that would labor to avoid the rigidities of a world government without abandoning international political sanctions. This would regulate world culture but not organize it. One of many solutions Satin offers is a system of planetary taxation on resource use which would be part of an economic redistribution of wealth to poorer nations.[20] Although the planet must be unified economically, politically and socially, Satin and many New Age political thinkers such as Marilyn Ferguson strongly support the decentralization of civil government. Government must be made manageable and reduced to a more "human scale." Here much of the New Age follows economist E. F. Schumacher's idea that "small is beautiful."

## Putting the One to Work

The idea of having one world government is far from merely theoretical. A host of organizations are energetically implementing the goal of a new world order. This should not be surprising since this ideal is not new with the New Age. H. G. Wells advocated a politically unified world in his many novels and essays and even outlined a strategy for its gradual advancement in his book *The Open Conspiracy* (1925). While many New Age thinkers shy away from Wells's notion of a ruling scientific elite, his thinking on world order is far from obsolete.[21] More than a few political groups stand in his shadow.

Planetary Citizens is one group dedicated to the transformation of the world through political action. Founded in 1972 by Donald Keys, a long-time consultant to United Nations delegations and committees, Planetary Citizens has attracted a huge and impressive roster of leaders—such as New Age luminaries David Spangler and Peter Caddy (both formerly of Findhorn community), William Irwin Thompson, Willis Harman (futurist), Edgar Mitchell (ex-astronaut) and Michael Murphy (of Esalen Institute). Distinguished members have included Isaac Asimov, René Dubos and the current honorary chairman Norman Cousins.

Humanity, says Keys, is "on the verge of something entirely new, a further evolutionary step unlike any other: the emergence of the first global civilization."[22] We are advancing toward "Omega," which, according to Teilhard de Chardin, would mean the unification of consciousness and culture. Leading the "passage to planetization," Keys contends, is the New Consciousness movement, represented by communities such as Findhorn, growth centers like Esalen, the Association for Humanistic Psychology and others that will "offer a major venue for myths which will form and inform the emergent world order."[23] Keys calls the United Nations the "nexus of emerging planetary values," and he hopes it will establish a "planetary management system."[24]

In early 1982 Planetary Citizens and several other groups kicked off a consciousness-raising project called "Planetary Initiative for the World We Choose," a "coalition effort which involve[d] literally hundreds of groups and organizations, large and small, worldwide."[25] Keys viewed it as a coming-out party for the New Age which had previously not been organized in political events. Study groups were formed, a newspaper called *The Initiator* was published and much attention was drawn to the world order movement.

The Initiative culminated in a Planetary Congress in Toronto in June of 1983. Nearly five hundred people (including New Age notables Barbara Marx Hubbard and Ram Dass) from twenty countries met for the four-day event.[26] The congress published its results in *The Initiator* as the "Declaration on the World We Choose." The document covered a gamut of topics concerning ecology, economics, politics and so on. The New Age orientation, I think, was obvious. It sees as pivotal to "a fulfilling and harmonious future" the need to achieve "the individual human potential and . . . the essential spiritual identity of each person, giving rise to a oneness with all life."[27] It also trumpeted the need for a new economic order, a stronger United Nations and a centralized global government.

Another political lobby, World Goodwill, shares nearly all the goals of Planetary Citizens. Like Planetary Citizens, it is headquartered on United Nations Plaza near the organization it heralds as the agent of world peace and order. Its aim is to unfold "the Plan" as spelled out in the many books of Alice Bailey, particularly *The Externalization of the Hierarchy* (1957).

Bailey claimed her works were telepathically received from "the Tibetan" Djwhal Khul. Khul predicted a new world government and world religion to be galvanized by "the reappearance of the Christ." This Christ is not Jesus Christ of the Bible but an advanced member of a spiritual hierarchy whose reappearance must be summoned by "The Great Invocation," a prayer widely distributed by Bailey's followers. Bailey expected the New Age to dawn after a global crisis occurred which could be rectified only by "the Christ." But, she believed, we can offset our present futility and frustration and find incentive toward building a new world through the belief in the essential divinity of humanity. A "new world religion" will result, eclipsing traditional Christianity.[28]

This world view remains only slightly below the surface of World

Goodwill's activities and information. The group itself is one of several Bailey-oriented groups sponsored by the Lucis Trust, a long-standing occult organization originally called the Lucifer Trust which came about when Bailey broke from Theosophy.

A student of Bailey's teachings, Benjamin Creme, heralded the immanent reappearance of the Christ (whom he called Maitreya) in the late seventies and early eighties. Claiming to be telepathically "overshadowed" by the Christ, Creme would give transmissions from his master on a variety of vital subjects concerning spirituality and politics.[29] Creme, a middle-aged English occultist, helped lead a worldwide advertising campaign designed to prepare the world for the Christ and to demonstrate the need to invoke him through "The Great Invocation." The Tara Center placed ads in major newspapers worldwide announcing the great revelation that would lead to the end of world hunger, war and strife. The result would be a one-world socialist government largely dependent on the redistribution of wealth by the United Nations. The Great Invocation even appeared in an ad in _The Reader's Digest_ in October of 1982. But despite the messianic hoopla, the Christ refused to reappear, a fact predictably blamed on humanity's lack of invocative power.

Another New Age world-order activist is Robert Muller who has served in the United Nations for over thirty years, currently as its assistant secretary-general. His concern for a "global spirituality" has made him popular on the New Age circuit. Announcing an impending "cosmic age" wherein we will become "the planet of God," he sees humankind on a universal scale "seeking no less than its reunion with the 'divine,' its transcendence into ever higher forms of life." He then commends the Hindus who "rightly see no difference between our earth and the divine."[30] The United Nations, he believes, has been and will be a decisive catalyst for global transformation.

**New Age Impact**
Forms of New Age politics range from the eccentric to the plausible,

from occult idealism to skillful political pragmatism. The number of groups involved and issues covered is far too great for our discussion; but the fact remains that a growing number of theorists and activists are stumping for the One, whether it be in the area of world order, ecology, feminism, disarmament or the teaching of meditation in the public schools. But how can this eclectic group of idealists make a difference? Can they wield political power?

New Age political unity is not so much organizational as it is ideological. Ferguson notes that the collusion in New Age politics is in its assumptions.[31] This collusion of assumptions is maintained, strengthened and implemented through networking. Rather than relying on a formal organization, the New Age seeks to find connections through a web of informational networks which Ferguson believes will "generate power enough to remake society."[32] The strategy is to link groups and individuals through "conferences, phone calls, air travel, books, phantom organizations, papers, pamphleteering, photocopying, lectures, workshops, parties, grapevines, mutual friends, summit meetings, coalitions, tapes, [and] newsletters"[33] in a web of influence which is at once expansive, powerful, decentralized and intimate. A glance through *The New Consciousness Source Book, The New Age Directory* or other such books will show how broad the movement is.

It is difficult to gauge the success of New Age politics. Many of those who agree with New Age concerns (global unity, ecology, feminism and so on) may not share the pantheistic world view. Yet New Age ideas are finding their way into civil government and receiving our tax dollars.

One prominent area of influence is the Congressional Clearinghouse on the Future, a legislative service organization designed to aid congress in assessing major trends affecting the future. This congressional caucus, organized in 1976, keeps politicians abreast of the latest thinking in futures research on a variety of issues from many perspectives. It publishes newsletters and organizes lectures and dialogs with such New Age activists as Fritjof Capra, Hasel Henderson, Marilyn Ferguson, Jeremy Rifkin and John Naisbett, thus providing a governmentally sponsored forum for New Age approaches.[34]

Politicians and political parties are catching the transformationalist contagion. *The Leading Edge Bulletin,* a New Age paper addressing social transformation, carried the headline, " 'Transformation' planks become part of Democratic platform." Members of the Association for Humanistic Psychology and the New World Alliance analyzed previous California Democratic platforms and drafted amendments they sought to include in newer platforms. Much of the wording of "The Transformation Platform," a document created by the New World Alliance, was finally included in the 1982 California Democratic platform. The text concludes with a statement agreeable to any New Age advocate: "Ultimately, all humanity must recognize the essential interconnectedness and interdependence of all human beings and all of nature—humanity has no other choice if we are to stop world annihilation."[35] This is not to imply that the Democratic Party is in itself New Age, but simply to show an area of influence.

Several politicians embody New Age values, perhaps most notably Jerry Brown, ex-governor of California and aspirant for the Democratic presidential nomination in 1980. Barbara Marx Hubbard, a futurist and prominent spokeswoman for the New Age, waged a political campaign for the Democratic vice-presidency in 1984.

New Age politics is also gaining currency outside the United States. According to the New Age newsletter *Renewal,* Sweden is the first country where "transformation oriented politics have entered the political mainstream." The Swedish government sponsored a conference called "Living Companies in the New Age" that drew five hundred people, mostly corporate executives, to hear New Age thinkers Hasel Henderson, Elisabeth Kübler-Ross, Carl Rogers and like-minded Scandinavian transformationalists. The government-run Secretariat for Future Studies serves as an ongoing catalyst for implementing New Age ideas.[36]

The Green Party of Germany is a young but growing political force which also embodies many New Age viewpoints. The Green agenda challenges traditional politics by emphasizing issues such as ecology, feminism, antinuclear and peace issues. Manon Maren-Grisenbaach, who served for two years on the Green's national executive committee, explains their ecological vision: "The emphasis on relations and interconnections—in Gregory Bateson's words, 'the pattern which connects the crab to the lobster and the orchid to the primrose and all four of them to me'—is the foundation of Green thought and being."[37] Capra and Spretnak share the Green vision and have written a book about it, *Green Politics: The Global Premise* (1984). They point out the rise of "Green politics" throughout the world, hoping to inspire its ascendancy.

## Defense and Education

Ferguson notes that "research projects on meditation, biofeedback, psychic phenomena, and alternative medical approaches have been funded by the Department of Defense." Such funding, she thinks, gives legitimacy to ideas "that might otherwise appear 'far out.' "[38] One such case is the First Earth Battalion, the brainchild of a less than traditional military think tank. The battalion, also called the Natural Guard, is projected to be a New Age militia of warrior-monks, spiritually attuned to new methods of conflict resolution through yoga, meditation and the martial arts. Inner strength through the transformation of consciousness is the key. Its operations manual, "Evolutionary Tactics," says that "God is within each of us" and that the warrior-monk should develop "psiwork" which will involve the ability to read others' minds, spiritually leave the physical body, engage in psychokinesis and even pass through objects.[39] While it is not yet known if the battalion will ever get its feet on the earth, its key innovator, Jim Channon, was funded by the United States Army to produce a multimedia presentation on the battalion that was shown to the senior class of the United States Military Academy.

New Age ideas and practices are also infiltrating state-sponsored education. As we saw earlier, "confluent education," developed by Beverly Galyean, was introduced into the California curriculum, even though it is based on pantheistic theology.[40] Although Galyean is now deceased, New Age oriented education lives on. Project GOAL (Guidance Opportunities for Affective Learning) was developed in the early 1980s with federal and state funds to help handicapped children in Irvine, California. As of June 1982, it was also used in teaching non-handicapped children in all seventeen of Irvine's district elementary schools and in thirty-seven other districts.[41] The program includes yoga, biofeedback and guided imagery. Part of its game plan is "to introduce the children to the Inner Self—the self that can guide them in making decisions or in knowing what is true and good."[42]

Transcendental meditation tried for several years to introduce its ideas into public education until a court ruling in 1977 declared it a religious practice and thus in violation of the separation of church and state. Despite this, some state universities teach yoga through the physical education departments. Such initiation into the One is sponsored by all citizens through taxation.

Mark Satin's "New Age Political Platform," while advocating the repeal of all compulsory education laws, supports the use of " 'humanistic' and 'transpersonal' methods of teaching . . . that can develop our higher selves, as well as our intellects." He also encourages yoga and other Eastern practices for physical training.[43] Unless Satin wants to dismantle state-sponsored education entirely—which is unlikely—I think we may assume that he and others will use the political process to incorporate these practices into the public schools.

A host of other New Age political action groups could be mentioned, along with numerous reports of New Age ideas infiltrating civil government and the political process in general. Which groups will effectively infiltrate the state's infrastructure and which will become New Age Edsels is difficult to determine. If the philosophy of the One continues to expand and deepen its cultural credibility, the "new paradigm" will, as Ferguson notes, have the power to politicize "even those who have had no interest in conventional politics."[44]

In reflecting on possible hostility to "the new consciousness culture" by the "dominant 'straight' society," Donald Keys muses that the New Age would be an elusive enemy because of its widely decentralized strategies. The New Age emphasis on "the good old pioneering American virtues of self-reliance, thrift, self-discipline, and good neighborliness [would] nullify in advance charges of deviation from desirable norms."[45] If the One can skillfully retain a connection with traditional American political sensitivities while energizing them with a pantheistic vitality ("God is within; we can do it!") and technological ingenuity (networking), New Age politics may well color the future.

## Faulty Foundations

The sword of biblical evaluation must be laid to the roots of New Age politics. The entire political structure of the New Age is built on the sands of spiritual error. Although Christians may agree with certain proposals in the New Age agenda, the presuppositional antithesis between Christ and the One could not be sharper. The hope of the New Age in all its manifestations is in human potential, the divine within, the One for all. But as one astute reviewer of Capra's *The Turning Point* put it:

> Human ingenuity in creating untold misery did not wait for the development of a mechanistic world-view. . . . The holistic worldviews that have for thousands of years dominated thought in the far East have not avoided hunger, violence, overpopulation, nor the cultural revolution.[46]

While the Christian believes that political realism must begin with the fact of individual and corporate sin, the New Age recklessly invests hope in the release of innate human potential which it sees as inherently good and trustworthy. Present problems are solved by a holistic world view.

But sin is too stubborn to be dislodged by merely a change of perspective. The New Age equates sin with ignorance, and enlightenment with pantheism—the realization that all is one and all is god. Biblical faith sees such "enlightenment" as a counterfeit and a deception. Consciousness, whether personal or political, can never truly be raised unless it is first lowered to see the reality of sin and the need for redemption in Christ. All detours around the cross of Christ crash on the brutal rocks of reality. The Christian who yearns for political justice looks to God as Lord, Law-giver and Judge, not to the godhead within.

Both Mark Satin and Jerry Rubin speak of legitimate mystical experiences where good and evil dissipate into the One.[47] Ferguson claims that good and evil are transcended by an awareness that "unites opposites."[48] This moral uncertainty can be seen as well in Thompson's visionary treatise, *From Nation to Emanation*. Thompson tries to transcend all ideologies by appealing to the unification and equality of opposites. Good is not opposed to evil, but is in reciprocal interaction with it, both cosmically and politically. But what, then, is left of ethics?

The New Age is morally unfit to lead us politically. It lacks any absolute standard that would tell us that the outcome of the great transformation would be more good than evil. (Its general acceptance of the unbiblical and immoral practice of legalized abortion on demand, for example, is a key indication that its moral foundations are insecure.) Although eloquently expressed and elaborately constructed, in Thompson's system, for example, the only point of reference for any of his judgments is the planet itself. He closes his book by saying that "our planet is a crystalline image of everything we need to know to endure and prevail."[49] The Christian looks to the creation to see God's glory, of course, but not to derive ethics. We must look beyond the creation to the Creator and to his unchanging ethical standards revealed in the Bible.

## One World Idolatry

Whether New Age politics looks to the United Nations or to other less-renowned world order groups such as the Club of Rome, the idea of a unified world order captures their interest. The age of independent nations is over; nations must be united and globally guided.

Yet this may not be the benign goal it appears to be. New Age politics sometimes demonstrates an occult elitism much opposed to the populism it claims. As we saw earlier, World Goodwill is based on the teachings of Alice Bailey and incorporates her notion of "heirarchy" into its goals.

David Spangler, board member of Planetary Initiative and much influenced by Alice Bailey, speaks of Lucifer as "in a sense the angel of man's inner evolution" who has a positive role (along with "the Christ") in advancing humanity's cosmic consciousness.[50] Both Spangler and Thompson agree that the new political order must be hierarchical. All are not fit to lead the planet into the New Age. Eventually a democracy will result where all are aware of their divinity and are attuned to the whole; until then "it is obvious that in conducting the affairs of a spiritual society one would not turn to those less attuned."[51] Despite the fact that Spangler, Thompson and other New Age thinkers ostensibly decry totalitarianism and planetary tyranny, their outlook condones it. Only those crowned with cosmic consciousness are fit to rule. The word of the One is divinized and therefore final. It is also beyond good and evil. One group has absolute power and sees itself as spiritually superior. Any student of history can see that this is a dangerous situation.

In many world-government scenarios suggested by the New Age, the United Nations plays a prominent role. Although the original purpose of the United Nations was not to usurp national sovereignty, Doug Bandow notes that the United Nations' recent policies are placing it at the international helm. "The UN is drifting away from the goal of establishing an international peaceful order . . . and is working instead to build a New International Economic Order in which the UN manages global resources."[52] Even though the United Nations cannot be considered a New Age institution, many of its present goals parallel those found in the New Age movement.

Christian realism demands that no one political institution claim total power. Since all people are sinners and imperfect, political power should be counterbalanced between various institutions and nations. A centralization of power (statism) in a fallen world is even more dangerous than current national diversity. To put one's hope for peace and prosperity into a world government and not God is the same idolatry committed by the builders of the tower of Babel (Gen 11:1–9).

The Christian political conscience must reject idolatrous internationalism with as much enthusiasm as it rejects any idolatrous nationalism. Christ is Lord—not the nation, not the planet. Global government, or what could be called "the cosmic state," must be rejected.[53]

Despite whatever good intentions the New Age world-order advocates may have, the logic of their position lays a blueprint for totalitarianism and tyranny. They proclaim the necessity of maintaining "unity in diversity" in the new world order. Yet the logic of pantheism and globalism opposes this ideal. Despite the desire for national distinctiveness within the new world order, a global government necessitates coercive control and power. If global government is to *govern*—and not merely *suggest*—it must implement its authority by economic or military intervention. Such intervention would override any national self-determination or autonomy. There is a recurring tendency in New Age politics to ignore the reality of collective human evil. They frequently underestimate both the coercive force it will take to maintain a world government and the evil intentions of many modern nation states, particularly the Soviet Union. For instance, a major emphasis of the Green Party has been unilateral nuclear disarmament—which many see as a sure invitation for Soviet conquest. G. K. Chesterton went so far as to say that "exactly in proportion as you turn monotheism into monism you turn it into despotism."[54]

Christ came not to unify at all costs but to divide truth from falsity, good from evil, light from darkness (Lk 12:49-53). Gary North comments that "the quest for a total unity in terms or principles other than those laid down in the Bible is a perverse quest. Unity is to be *ethical,* not egalitarian or humanistic."⁵⁵ Unity is a goal to be pursued according to biblical standards, not merely human aspirations for a counterfeit oneness that negates biblical truth.

Satan tempted Christ by offering him all the kingdoms of the world if Christ would only worship him. But Christ vetoed his political agenda by declaring, "Away from me, Satan! For it is written: 'Worship the Lord your God, and serve him only' " (Mt 4:8-10). Similarly, the New Age tempts us to believe that the kingdoms of this world can become ours if we bow down to the divinity within ourselves, instead of worshiping God. But just as Christ did not accept political power on Satan's false terms, neither should the modern world. After all, it was Satan himself who first tempted humanity by saying we would be "like God" if we refused to be submissive to divine authority (Gen 3:5-6).

## The Ruler of the Kings of the Earth

The future of New Age politics is uncertain; but as long as the One gains cultural ground it will seek to annex political territory. To do so effectively it must couch its terms in politically acceptable language and seek to use and infiltrate existing political systems. But despite this tactic, an occult underbelly can often be exposed. For just this reason Christians must guard against any illicit political compromises and forge a consistent Christian critique and counterproposal.

The political world desperately thirsts for new life and ideological vigor. But the transfusion of the One into its veins will only reanimate the old humanistic hulk that beats its rugged and worn fists against the City of God. New policies might replace the old, but the old lie remains intact: we are gods and need no divine authority; we control our own destiny.

Despite all rebellion, Christ remains "ruler of the kings of the earth"

(Rev 1:5). God warns all political imposters: "Therefore, you kings, be wise; be warned, you rulers of the earth. Serve the LORD with fear and rejoice with trembling. Kiss the Son, lest he be angry and you be destroyed in your way, for his wrath can flare up in a moment. Blessed are all who take refuge in him" (Ps 2:10–12).

# New Age Spirituality

## 7

NEW AGE SPIRITUALITY COMES IN A VARIETY OF PACKAGES: FROM ESTAB-lished Eastern religious groups to personal meditative practices, from occult rituals to a general belief in reincarnation. Beliefs considered exotic or bizarre twenty years ago have carved their way into the West's "plausibility structure." They are acceptable and even noncontroversial to many; and they are clearly antithetical to orthodox Christianity.

This new spirituality is not necessarily reducible to the classical Eastern religions (Buddhism, Taoism, Hinduism and their offshoots). Rather, the injection of Eastern, neo-pagan and occult ideas into Western religious thought has produced a hybrid spirituality; it takes the essence of Eastern religions but retains some elements of the Western, Judeo-Christian world view. What results is a mutation. The One remains, but it is couched in certain Western sensibilities. Harvey

Cox's comment is fitting: "The end result of the Western prismatic refraction of the light from the East is a wholly new pattern."[1]

The West's and especially North America's concern with efficiency and immediate results has shaped this new spirituality. Because the modern lifestyle is characterized by quick and easy transitions in our pluralistic culture (changing churches, jobs, spouses or world views), commitment to a spiritual path must be streamlined and systematized. Although some may retreat to a Buddhist monastery or join a New Age commune, the new spiritual practices and beliefs are often geared specifically for modern life. Maharishi Mahesh Yogi's transcendental meditation, for instance, is presented as an efficient science of consciousness: follow the prescription (meditate twice daily, twenty minutes each time) and watch the results. Est offered its graduates enlightenment after only two intensive weekend seminars.

The One may even receive technological support. A California firm is marketing "samadhi tanks," sensory deprivation tanks that can be installed in the privacy of your own home. The purpose is to achieve a higher state of consciousness—"samadhi" is a Hindu term for "oneness with the One"—through entering a casketlike box which keeps out all light and noise while floating the user in water to simulate weightlessness. Supposedly, the mind turns inward and, through altered consciousness, produces various latent psychic powers.[2]

While some critics within the New Age may condemn such efficiency and pragmatism, the One often finds itself at home in this modern mindset. The agonized spiritual acrobatics of the mystics, masters and sages is bypassed in favor of "the American way." Harvey Cox refers to this attitude as "enlightenment by Ticketron."[3] The New Age repudiates the world-denying or ascetic approach that characterizes much of Eastern mysticism. Instead it favors a world-affirming or even hedonistic lifestyle where "enlightenment" is fully compatible with worldly success.

Western optimism and belief in progress pervade the new spirituality—something often foreign to classical Eastern religions. The theory of evolution is invested with mystical potency, as we saw in chapter one. Noted New Age scholar Ken Wilber confesses: "I really trust evolution. I really don't think God would screw us around that bad."[4] Our present crisis is seen as generating incredible opportunity.

The New Age spirituality is also bolstered by avant-garde theories on "the frontiers of science." Western respect for science has influenced many people to take seriously the claims that quantum physics, holographic theory or other scientific ideas should push us into the One's lap. New Age spirituality is not an island of personal mystical experience isolated from scientific concerns; it often looks to science for inspiration and confirmation, as is evidenced by the popularity of Capra's *The Tao of Physics.*

In charting New Age spirituality many people get off track by looking only at particular controversial cults. The membership and direct influence of pantheistic groups such as Eckankar, Church Universal and Triumphant (Elizabeth Clare Prophet), the Theosophical Society, transcendental meditation and others are actually much less than most people think.[5] Yet the influence of the New Age's spirituality goes far beyond highly dedicated members of specific groups.

## The New Pagans

Several cars at the University of Oregon in Eugene sport the bumper sticker "Pagan and Proud" or "I'm a Born-Again Pagan." Walking through the student union one day I was given a tract entitled, "A Pledge to Pagan Spirituality," which read in part:

I am a pagan and I dedicate myself to channeling the Spiritual Energy of my Inner Self to help and to heal myself and others.

* I know that I am a part of the Whole of Nature. May I grow in my understanding of the Unity of all Nature. . . . May I always be mindful that I create my own reality and that I have the power within me to create positivity in my life.

* May I always be mindful that the Goddess and God in all their forms dwell within me and that this divinity is reflected through

my own Inner Self, my Pagan Spirit. (Unsigned)

A trip to a local New Age or occult bookstore will reveal a host of books on pagan festivals, American Indian spirituality, witchcraft (Wicca), Egyptian religion and other pagan subjects. Evidence of a resurging interest in the pagan and the occult is appearing everywhere.

For many of us, the word *occult* conjures up images of the demonic and Satanic. Satanism, black masses and gruesome ritual sacrifice quickly come to mind. Although these elements have not been lacking in history and are not absent from the modern scene,[6] the burgeoning neo-pagan movement is not occult *in that sense*. While witchcraft is usually (and sometimes correctly) thought to be associated with Satan worship, many modern witches do not even believe in Satan.[7] Despite disbelief in Satan, however, the essence of occultism remains. *Occult* means "hidden" or "secret"; a concealed wisdom must be experienced for personal liberation and psychic power. Beyond the ordinary perceptions and feelings lies the experience of oneness, of the divine within. Connected with this monistic idea may be forms of divination (astrology, *I Ching*, tarot cards), spirit contact (with the dead, Ascended Masters or nature spirits) or psychic powers (telepathy, ESP, precognition, telekinesis, magic).

## The Great Goddess

Many people dissatisfied with the atrophied spirituality of the West have by-passed Christianity entirely in favor of a pre-Christian nature religion. According to Margot Adler, a priestess in a coven and a reporter for National Public Radio,

By *pagan* they [the pagans] usually mean the pre-Christian nature religions of the West, and their own attempts to revive them or to recreate them in new forms. The modern Pagan resurgence includes the new feminist goddess-worshipping groups, certain new religions based on the visions of science fiction writers, attempts to revive ancient European religions—Norse, Greek, Roman—and the surviving tribal religions.[8]

In rejecting much of Western culture—including established religion, male dominance, alienation from nature and the body—neo-pagans embrace the old ways of the earth and body. Through ritual, celebration and myth they attempt to reharmonize themselves with the Whole, or the One, which many of the groups refer to as the *Goddess.*

Patriarchal religion, these neo-pagans declare, pushed divinity off into the clouds and away from earth and heart; it deified masculinity and thus demoralized femininity, establishing male exploitation of women and nature. The Goddess, in all her ancient forms—Isis, Diana, Cubele, Hecate—symbolized the primal energies of fertility, sensuality, imagination and celebration. But Mother-earth was replaced by Father-God; cosmology and theology were fumigated of femininity, and for centuries God the Father and the *sons* of God ruled civilization after civilization. But now we must move "beyond God the Father" and be nurtured by the Goddess.[9]

Interest in the ancient Goddess religion ranges from those motivated to psychologically reform the Western male-dominated psyche with the potent symbolism and mythology of the ancients, to those who make Goddess worship a religious practice, often aligning it with feminist concerns. The various Goddesses of ancient culture serve as symbols of liberation from spiritual inferiority and personal and political powerlessness. Goddess enthusiasts usually advocate either the superiority of women or some kind of androgenous ideal.

The revival of witchcraft (also known as Wicca) represents the return to the Goddess. While traditional male-dominated religion suppressed the Goddess in its theology and witch hunting, the Goddess will again prevail. The hope is that the old, deceptive view of witchcraft as demonic and Satanic will give way to the positive evaluation that Wicca is a natural spirituality of ecological wholeness and pantheistic pleasures. A modern witch said in an interview that "paganism is the spirituality of the ecological movement."[10] According to Starhawk, a modern witch, "The Goddess . . . *is* the world. Manifest in each of us, She can be known by every individual, in all her magnificent diversity. . . . Religion is a matter of relinking, with the divine within and with her outer manifestations in all of the human and natural world."[11]

Goddess worshipers come together in covens to practice "the craft" and to kindle the "Goddess within." Witches believe that by attuning themselves with the (one) Goddess, they can use magic (spell-casting and so on) to achieve their ends. Coven meetings often involve various rituals, including group chanting and sometimes nudity.[12] The monistic nature of magic is seen in Starhawk's explanation:

> The primary principle of magic is connection. The universe is a fluid, ever-changing energy pattern, not a collection of fixed and separate things. What affects one thing affects, in some way, all things: All is interwoven into the continuous fabric of being. Its warp and weft are energy, which is the essence of magic.[13]

For Starhawk, we "are all psychic, unconsciously," and she gives us various exercises for awakening this power.[14]

While Goddess worship can be seen as a return to a pre-Christian form of religion, historical accuracy does not seem to be highly valued. Rosemary Ruether, writing in *The Christian Century,* questions much of the feminist scholarship regarding the existence and role of the Goddess in history, seeing it as simplistic and ideologically limited: "A tendentious use of historical material reduces everything to one drama: the story of original female power and goodness, and evil male conquest and suppression of the same."[15] She points out that the *presence* of female deities in the past may not have meant their dominance.[16] Many Goddess worshipers, I think, disparage accurate historical research as superfluous. Z Budapest, a practicing witch, has said, "After all, if Goddess religion is sixty thousand years old or seven thousand, it does not matter. Certainly not for the future! Recognizing the divine Goddess within is where real religion is at."[17] While not all the Goddess scholarship is so affected, the attitude in Goddess writings is often more concerned to create a new symbolism and mythology than to unearth a historical precedent.

## Other Neo-Pagan Ideas

The Goddess religion has gained influence because of its alignment with feminism, but it is not the only expression of neo-paganism active today. A detailed listing and analysis of the many groups and philosophies is beyond our scope, but I will briefly mention a few of these other manifestations of this movement.

Interest and involvement in ancient, pre-Christian religions often center on the shamanistic traditions of the world. Ken Wilber comments that "the true shaman was the first voyager into the realms of the superconscious,"[18] meaning that the ancient seers began to discover the ultimate oneness. The shaman is "a technician of ecstasy," whose purpose is to reconnect people with the sacred, as mystic mediator, guide and healer.

Michael Harner, author of *The Way of the Shaman* (1982), began studying shamanism as an anthropological observer; he is now a shaman himself. I saw him address a large, very receptive group of university students who were fascinated by his reports of mystical visions and encounters with various spiritual entities. His book outlines how shamanistic techniques can transport one into the spiritual world through a change of consciousness. His seminars on shamanism focus on the interrelationship of the human, animal and spiritual realms. The approach is a blend of animism (spirit contact) and pantheism: by becoming a kind of shaman one may harmonize the spiritual and natural worlds within oneself. Psychic abilities may be cultivated and utilized. The many books of Carlos Castaneda concerning American Indian sorcery have done much to trigger interest in shamanism. No longer looked down on as "medicine men" or "pagans," the shamans are viewed by many as spiritual masters.

Another very popular and influential example of the animist-pantheist resurgence is the Findhorn community of northern Scotland. Although now declining somewhat in influence, Findhorn enamored a host of spiritual sojourners by its tales of miraculously large garden plants grown in the most inhospitable conditions, as well as accounts of visitations with nature spirits (devas) and assorted other spiritual entities.[19] During the sixties and seventies, Findhorn served as Mecca and model for the New Age community. Mixing occultism, animism, Eastern religions and other ingredients, Findhorn made the animistic-pantheistic world view palatable and intriguing.

To our list of neo-pagan philosophies we could add druidism, Celtic spirituality, Egyptian religion and any number of tribal and indigenous forms of animism and pantheism. Although these groups do not draw their spirituality primarily from the East, their world view and religious practices converge on the One. Margot Adler, in her extensive study of neo-paganism, sees the pagan world view as essentially polytheistic-pantheistic. The One takes many forms, but remains the same underneath it all.

> No matter how diverse the Neo-Pagan's ideas about deities, almost all of them have some kind of "Thou Art God/dess" concept. . . . Most would agree that the goal of Neo-Paganism is, in part, to become what we potentially are, to become "as the gods," or, if we are God/dess, to recognize it, to make our God/dess-hood count for something.[20]

The pantheon of gods and goddesses are but symbolic representations of the One reality, the totality of Nature. Divinity is sought within the self—which is really nothing but the cosmic self (the One) in disguise.

The neo-pagan world view and many of its practices are becoming commonplace. Gordon Melton, director of the Institute for the Study of American Religion, estimates that some thirty thousand people in North America celebrated the Goddess on Halloween in 1982.[21] Theodore Roszak dismisses the criticism that the neo-pagan "ritual improvisations and mythological variations are often based on some shaky historical speculation" by affirming that they are speaking to "the present needs of our culture" and with a "power greater than their own." They live out what would otherwise only be academic theories of pre-Christian religion.[22]

## Beyond God the Father?

Christianity is often criticized for being sexist. Some, like the neo-pagan feminists, claim that a male Deity leads directly to the male oppression of females in society. Yet this is a distortion of the biblical view. The Bible values highly both women and men.

Since God is not human, he is neither male nor female in the sexual sense; he is beyond human sexuality but not beyond personality. Carl Henry helps clarify the issue:

> In sharp distinction from the ancient Near Eastern fertility cults and their nature gods, the Bible studiously avoids imputing sexual organs to God even anthropomorphically. Feminine and masculine sexual elements are excluded from both the Old and New Testament doctrine of deity. The God of the Bible is a sexless God. When Scripture speaks of God as "he" the pronoun is primarily personal (generic) rather than masculine (specific); it emphasizes God's personality . . . in contrast to impersonal entities.[23]

Male imagery of God in the Bible neither depreciates women nor excludes feminine traits from God's character. Both men and women are made in God's image (Gen 1:26) for a relationship of mutual support and encouragement, not of superiority and inferiority. God alone is the true superior and final Lord.

The Bible doesn't avoid feminine images for God. Jesus likens God to a loving and saddened mother hen crying over the waywardness of her children (Mt 23:37-39). God is also said to have "given birth" to Israel (Deut 32:18; see also Is 42:14; 46:3; 49:15; 66:13; Ps 131:2).

Yet God is never referred to as "she." The actions of God are sometimes described in feminine terms, but never is the person of God described as feminine. The Bible speaks of God *the Father.* Jesus taught his disciples to pray "Our Father, who art in heaven . . ." God our mother is not mentioned.[24] As Susan Foh says, "For the father-hood of God to be significant, there must be a difference between fatherhood and motherhood."[25]

Yet mothers and fathers are not different in their essential person-hood, but according to their functions in parenting. God is the perfect Father; and if the Bible is inspired by God, we should not dispense with the imagery that he has given; as C. S. Lewis said, "God himself has taught us how to speak of Him."[26]

The crux of the matter is that God is not impersonal. For even in the feminist Goddess religions, the Goddess is not really a person at all, but merely a personification of the One. The biblical metaphors of God refer to a person; Goddess metaphors speak of feminine at-tributes but refer to the impersonal matrix or principle of existence rather than to a personal female deity ruling the universe. The God-dess is not above all as ruler or lord, but the All itself, "the maternal ground of being."[27] She is nothing but a literary device to evoke interest. "She" doesn't even exist; only "It" (the One) exists. The throne room of the universe is thus left empty.

## Eastern Religions

As already mentioned, the migration of Eastern religious ideas to the West often results in their adaptation to Western thinking. It is im-possible to list or adequately summarize the various forms of Eastern spirituality, so we shall limit ourselves to exploring the essence of Eastern religion and its appeal.

Hinduism is a religion of diverse faces—some polytheistic, some theistic and some pantheistic.[28] Likewise, Buddhism is made up of a variety of schools ranging from atheistic to pantheistic. Despite these internal differences, there is a general agreement within much of the Eastern tradition that there exists an all-encompassing oneness and that the person is identified with the whole. This spirit of oriental religion differs substantially from Christianity in that it blurs or oblit-erates the distinction between the Creator and the creation. In Hinduism the statement "that art thou" refers to the unity of subject and object, knower and known, human and God. All is really Brahman (the One). A passage from the Chandogya Upanishad (Hindu Scripture) illustrates this: "Though you do not see Brahman in this body, he is indeed here. That which is the subtle essence—in that have all things their existence. That is the truth. That is the Self. And that, Svetaketu, THAT ART THOU."[29]

One's ignorance of "that art thou" is a problem of perception, of forgetting one's true identity. The basic problem to be overcome in the Eastern systems is the illusion of separation and individuality. We get caught in the world of appearances (maya) and miss our oneness with the One. Yet the One remains. As the Chandogya Upanishad goes on to say:

He who knows, meditates upon, and realizes this truth of the Self, finds that everything—primal energy, ether, fire, water, and all other elements—mind, will, speech, sacred hymns and scriptures—indeed the whole universe—issues forth from it.

It is written: *He who has realized eternal Truth does not see death, nor illness, nor pain; he sees everything as the Self, and obtains all.*[30]

Experiential knowledge of the true Self releases us from illusion and the cycle of reincarnation. In Hinduism the experience of oneness with the One may be called *moksha, satchidananda* or *samadhi;* in Buddhism it is *nirvana* or *satori.* According to Bhagwan Shree Rajneesh, a popular and controversial Indian guru with a large Western following, "moksha is not freedom of the self, but freedom from the self. Moksha is selflessness. I am not a self, nor is anyone else a self."[31] Through meditation, he says, "you will be tuned to the infinite, then you will be tuned to the cosmic—then you will be one with the whole."[32]

This is pantheistic monism: all is god; all is one; "that art thou." Despite variations, the basic assumption is that there is no ultimate distinction between humanity and deity. This reality may be called many things—Brahman, Atman, the Void—but is at base the same: the One for all.

The One is found and experienced through a process of self-discovery, whether it be meditation, yoga or some other spiritual discipline. Ken Wilber, himself a student of Zen Buddhism, believes that some kind of Eastern meditation is crucial:

> If we—you and I—are to further the evolution of mankind . . . if we are to help the overcoming of our self-alienation from Spirit and not merely perpetuate it, then meditation—or a similar truly contemplative practice—becomes an absolute ethical imperative, a new categorical imperative.[33]

The classic Western spirituality of prayer, faith and obedience to an external God must be replaced by monistic meditation, personal experience and the God within. Eastern meditative practices emphasize emptying the mind of the illusion of separation and dualistic thinking. A holy word (mantra) may be repeated in order to change one's consciousness. Various special postures (as in yoga) are also employed for this end. The goal is an experience of unity with all things, the dissolution of the individual self and the discovery of the "divine within."

When the Bible speaks of meditation it means rumination on God and his Word: a filling of the mind with God's truth. Vain, irrational repetitions are excluded (Mt 6:7). Psalm 1 says that the person who delights "in the law of the LORD" and "meditates" on it "day and night" is "like a tree planted by streams of water, which yields its fruit in season and whose leaf does not wither" (vv. 2-3). Psychologist Carl Jung noted the great difference between a Christian meditation and the Eastern view. He says, "The Christian during contemplation would never say '*I* am Christ,' but will confess with Paul: 'Not I, but Christ liveth in me' (Gal 2:20). Our sutra [Buddhist writing] however says: 'Thou will know that *thou* art the Buddha.' "[34]

Theism's contention that God must be addressed, worshiped and obeyed as a personal Creator distinct from the creation is seen by the

New Age as a deficient spirituality. As Wilber puts it, at the highest level of consciousness, "saintly communion with spirit is transcended by sagely identity with spirit."[35] God is beyond personality; only those less advanced view him as a person. Rajneesh cautions that there is no relationship in or with the divine. A relationship takes at least two people; but *all* is one. He says: "The divine has no self so you cannot be related to it. A bhakti, a devotee, can never reach the divine because he thinks in terms of relationship: God the Father, God the lover, God the beloved . . . he goes on thinking of God as other."[36]

God, in many of the religions of the East, is also beyond rationality. Average, rational consciousness is only concerned with appearances and dualisms—humanity and nature, God and humanity, person and person—but logic cannot describe the One; it is beyond the scope of dualistic reason. To those Westerners tired of arid rationalism and intellectual disappointments, the One beyond reason may come as a welcome alternative. For example, many of Rajneesh's followers come from well-educated European and American backgrounds, while Rajneesh himself teaches people to distrust reason and to pass into an experience beyond it. Certainly not all New Age teachers hold this view of reason—some speak of transcending logic without abandoning it[37]—but most agree that the divine reality must be experienced by some means other than normal thought processes.

If the scope of dualistic reason cannot encompass the One, neither can moral reasoning. Traditional Western thought divides ethical considerations into good and evil, right and wrong, helpful and harmful; but if all is one, these dualisms must be dissolved. In summarizing the difference between East and West, Joseph Campbell clearly makes this point when he speaks of the oriental idea that

> the ultimate ground of being transcends thought, imagining, and definition. It cannot be qualified. Hence, to argue that God, Man, or Nature is good, just, merciful, or benign is to fall short of the question. One could just as appropriately—or inappropriately— have argued, evil, unjust, merciless, or malignant. All such anthro-

pomorphic predications screen or mask the actual enigma, which is absolutely beyond rational consideration.[38]

The *Bhagavad Gita* ("Song of God") is a sacred Scripture for Hindus and has become popular in the West. In it, Krishna, the manifestation of God, convinces Arjuna to fight in a battle that would kill some of his kinsmen. Krishna argues that there is really no death anyway; it is illusion. "That Reality which pervades the universe is indestructible. No one has the power to change the Changeless. Bodies are said to die, but That which possesses the body is eternal. It cannot be limited, or destroyed. Therefore you must fight."[39]

Beyond good and evil, beyond the changeable, lies the One. Swami Vivekananda, an early force in bringing Hinduism to America, saw God as both good and evil, for he is the All. As a fervent devotee of the goddess Kali (Hindu deity of destruction), he said, "Who can say that God does not manifest Himself as Evil as well as Good? But only the Hindu dares to worship him in the evil. . . . How few have dared to worship death, or Kali! Let us worship Death!" Viewing India as a source of spiritual revival in the West, he said that "the East must come to the West, not as sycophant, not as servant, but as Guru and teacher."[40]

## Jesus Goes East

As we said earlier, New Age spirituality takes on a distinctive Western identity. Because the West still remembers its Christian heritage, traffics in Christian images and bandies about Christian words, Christian symbols serve as a good medium for advancing the One. The semantic rail system has already been laid by hundreds of years of Christian tradition, and the message is now steaming full speed ahead.

One means of introducing pantheism in Christian terms is by reintroducing the heresy of Gnosticism. Elaine Pagels, whose book *The Gnostic Gospels* (1979) won the National Book Critics award, presents the early Gnostics as a persecuted minority and the representatives of a legitimate Christian tradition. Gnostics taught male-female equality and an androgenous God and saw knowledge of self as knowledge of God (unlike orthodoxy's emphasis on an external God). The orthodox had only faith, but the Gnostics had knowledge (gnosis): oneness with the One.

The Christ of the Bible taught that sin alienated people from a holy God; Gnosticism, in general, "insisted that ignorance, not sin, is what involves people in suffering."[41] The orthodox Christ announced himself as the Savior, the only way to be reconciled with God the Father; the Gnostic Christ disclosed secret wisdom (gnosis) that taught the disciples that they are divine as he is divine—"It is I who am the All."[42] He said: "He who will drink from my mouth will become like me. I myself shall become he."[43]

It is this Christ which the New Age seeks to place in its pantheon of monistic masters. One way the Christ of orthodoxy is reshaped is by speculating on the eighteen "lost years" of Jesus not elucidated in the Bible. During this time, from later childhood to adulthood, Jesus is said to have traveled to the East where he learned esoteric mysteries. Whether he made it to India or Persia or Tibet is debated but not crucial. Somehow he was initiated into the One.

In her popular autobiography Shirley MacLaine reports a conversation with a friend in which he discourses about the true Christ who "became an adept yogi and mastered complete control over his body and the physical world around him." Christ "tried to teach people that they could do the same things if they got more in touch with their spiritual selves and their own potential power."[44] According to Western yogi Christopher Hills, "Christ had trained as a great Siddha yogi with the powers of consciousness of a true initiate."[45] *The Aquarian Gospel of Jesus the Christ,* not an ancient gospel but one written from a vision given to "Levi" H. Downing, has Jesus saying, "The universal God is one, yet, he is more than one; all things are God; all things are one."[46] Jesus came not to free people from their sin but to "prove the possibilities of man."[47]

New Age writers often separate the historical person Jesus of Nazareth from the Christ or the Christ consciousness which Jesus attained—that is, found within himself. Jesus is not the God-man but one of many God-realized masters. According to David Spangler, "the Christ is that life, love, intelligence, energetic power which maintains creation in existence. It is within each one of us."[48] Christ's message becomes, "I am attuned, I am one with the whole."[49]

The true gospel of the One is thought to be the esoteric side of Christianity. *Exoteric* Christianity is the Westernized substitute and is barren of spiritual authenticity, expressing what Wilber calls "average-mode mentality."[50] *Esoteric* Christianity is in tune with "the perennial philosophy" of the One which manifests itself in all religious traditions. The New Age Christ stands against orthodox Christianity. Wilber sees Christ's understanding as transcending the Jewish monotheism of his day. He says, "Christ's revelation was an evolutionary advance, a revelation . . . that 'I and my Father are One.' . . . This was the same revelation that the Upanishads brought in India: *Tat tvam asi,* 'Thou art That,' you and God are ultimately one."[51]

## The New Age Christ on Trial

Before calling pantheism into question by comparing it with biblical Christianity, we must bring this New Age Christ to trial. If Christ is not one with the Hindus (and others), the One will have to find assistance elsewhere. Any world view worth its sociological salt must make an attempt to find some place for Jesus Christ. He demands attention. By sending him Eastward (during his "lost years"), many try to shine a new spotlight to illumine his identity. But can a case be made that he turned East? Does his teaching agree with pantheism?

First of all, the Bible itself cannot be construed as teaching the One for all. Jesus Christ stood firmly within the Jewish tradition of seeing God as Creator, distinct and above his creation. Jesus said he did not come to set aside the Old Testament, but to fulfill it (Mt 5:17-20). God is holy and people are to be holy also, but this is not a matter of finding God within or of becoming one with the One.

Nevertheless, New Age writers will sometimes quote Jesus' statement that "the kingdom of God is within you" (Lk 17:21) to mean that all people have "the divine within." But this interpretation is unfaithful to the text. The context shows Jesus answering a question asked by the Pharisees, members of the religious orthodoxy of the day. They wanted to know when the kingdom would come. Jesus answers that it is already here; that it is "within" you. Some translations have "among you" (an alternate translation in the NIV) or "in your midst" (NASB), meaning that the kingdom is present in Jesus and in those who follow him. Jesus constantly criticized the Pharisees for hypocrisy and spiritual blindness, and so he could not have been affirming that the kingdom was inherently or latently within them personally. We must also realize that he is not speaking of divinity ("the divine within") but of *the kingdom,* that is, the dynamic rule of God in the world.

Another passage sometimes quoted to support pantheism is John 10:22-42 where Jesus encounters Jews who wanted to stone him. In defending himself Jesus speaks of the Scripture that says, "You are gods" (Ps 82:6). This is interpreted by some New Age advocates to mean that Jesus asserted the divinity of all people. But Psalm 82 refers to the rulers of Israel, who were given divine jurisdiction to judge righteously according to God's law. Translations thus render *gods* (rulers) with a small g rather than a capital letter. This does not mean that all are God, but that the term *gods* was the title used to designate the Jewish rulers. Verse 7 makes this plain when it goes on to say that despite their divine appointment they "will die like mere men" and "fall like every other ruler." Jesus refers to this psalm to illustrate that he, like the earlier rulers, has authority from God the Father and that he should not be reproached for exercising it. Jesus is not saying, "Don't stone me for blasphemy because we're all gods anyway," but, "You are wrong to think that I should not claim authority as a ruler when this is exactly what the Old Testament says I should do." (In the overall context of the Bible, Jesus claims much more than this—for he is God incarnate—but not less than this.)

To assume that "the kingdom is within you" or "you are gods" really teaches pantheism is to engage in what James Sire calls "world view confusion": someone reads a certain world view into the text (in this case pantheism) which was not originally there. It ignores the cultural factors of the writer and his audience and so frees itself from the text's context and the author's intended meaning. In other words, by this method of interpretation one can make a text mean anything. This may make for imaginative apologetics, but it completely disregards the principles of proper interpretation of any human document, whether it be the Constitution, a Hindu holy book, a personal letter or the Bible.[52]

Undaunted by this argument, the New Age may claim that the traditional Bible is not a true record of what Christ taught and is therefore not to be trusted. We should rather look to the Gnostic records. But the attractiveness of the Gnostic records lies more in their agreement with modern New Age tastes than in their historical credibility. Much of the interest in these "lost Gospels" seems to be based on the idea that minority viewpoints should be favored. That is, since Gnosticism was suppressed and lost out historically, it must be somehow superior. This assumption, made by Elaine Pagels and others, also contends that Gnosticism was rejected because it threatened orthodoxy. It had to be suppressed for political and ecclesiastical reasons—not because it was theologically defective.

But other factors must be considered. Minorities are certainly often wrong. The novelty of any position does nothing to logically establish its truth. Gnosticism was and is a minority viewpoint. So is the theology of the Ku Klux Klan. This, in itself, proves nothing. But was the church afraid of Gnosticism? Or was Gnosticism simply not credible as a record of what the actual historical Jesus said and lived?

Much modern scholarship supports the historical credibility of the canonical Gospels as reliable records of what really happened.[53] The Gnostic Gospels, on the other hand, have little or no historical credibility. Biblical scholar Raymond Brown notes that while the title of Pagels's book, *The Gnostic Gospels,* "might lead us to anticipate new knowledge about the historical Jesus . . . we learn not a single verifiable fact about Jesus' ministry."[54] Although we cannot go into all the scholarly details, Joseph Fitzmyer and others have questioned Pagels's use of the Gnostic materials. Fitzmyer points out that many of the references in the book are not to *gospels* (supposed accounts of Christ's life) at all, but to the patristic (early church) writings. Other reviews accuse her of misinterpreting and popularizing the material by altering it to suit modern tastes.[55]

But what about the popular notion that Christ traveled to the East for inner wisdom and spiritual power? Although the Gnostic documents do not make this claim, it is nevertheless supposed by many New Agers. The Bible says nothing about Jesus traveling outside of Israel. It describes the "lost years" of his life with one verse: "And Jesus grew in wisdom and stature, and in favor with God and men" (Lk 2:52). This covers the time roughly between the ages of twelve and thirty, after which Jesus began his public ministry. Since the writers of the Gospels had been with Christ themselves or else had access to the best information about him, we can assume that they would have mentioned something as important as Jesus traveling outside of Israel. They do not.

Much of the thinking that Jesus did travel to Egypt, India, Persia or Tibet is based not on historical evidence but on mediumistic material, such as Levi's *Aquarian Gospel of Jesus the Christ* or Edgar Cayce's trance communications. The historical logic argues against such a claim, as Dave Hunt points out. Jesus was known not as a world traveler but as "the carpenter" (Mk 6:3) and "the carpenter's son" (Mt 13:55)—names that show he was known in the community over a period of time. He was not regarded as an exotic sage importing alien wisdom, but as a Jewish teacher who stunned his crowds with the radicalness of his teaching.[56]

The New Testament records that Jesus Christ fulfilled a score of Old

Testament prophecies concerning his birth, life, death and resurrection,[57] none of which mention any journey to the East. Rather, the
East came to him when the wise men (Magi), after spotting a star in
the East, traveled to Jerusalem to behold "the king of the Jews" (Lk
2:1–2). The only journey to the East mentioned in the Bible is the one
included in Christ's Great Commission to take the gospel to all nations (Mt 28:18–20).

### Reincarnation or Redemption?

Another area where the East has influenced the modern mindset is
in the growing belief in reincarnation. A 1982 Gallup Poll claimed that
twenty-three per cent of the American public believed in some form
of reincarnation.[58]

According to most Eastern thought, many lives are required to
reach oneness with the One; salvation is a multilifetime process of
progression or digression. If one accumulates good karma, positive
benefits accrue in later lives. Bad karma produces future punish-
ments. Eventually one may leave the cycle of birth and rebirth entirely
through the experience of enlightenment. Redemption, if it could be
called that, is a process of realizing the true self throughout many
lifetimes. According to Madame Blavatsky, founder of the Theosophical Society, "It is owing to this law of spiritual development that
mankind will become freed from its false gods and find itself finally—
SELF-REDEEMED."[59]

The Bible clearly rejects reincarnation as a doctrine of salvation:
"Man is destined to die once, and after that to face judgment" (Heb
9:27). But there are also some logical inconsistencies in the doctrine
of reincarnation. This growing belief sounds just and attractive at first
blush, but something else lies below the surface. First, the doctrine
as conceived in Hinduism and Buddhism involves all forms of life and
is called "transmigration." Westerners ignore this fact and color the
idea with hopes for self-development. But according to the Eastern
doctrine, one may come back as a dog, cow or gnat—something

decidedly less attractive than a more fully realized "human potential."

Second, the idea that reincarnation insures cosmic justice breaks down. If one is being punished or rewarded in this life for deeds in a previous life without the knowledge of that previous life, it is difficult to see how this could be interpreted as "just." How can one learn from or repent of sins which cannot even be remembered? Also, because of its monism, Eastern thought does not provide criteria for judging what deserves punishment and what deserves reward.

Third, popular opinion to the contrary, Eastern views of reincarnation do not stress a concrete soul or ego enduring through various lifetimes; the individual self is not real. How then can the system make sense if there is actually nothing to be reincarnated? And if something is reincarnated, then that something is impersonal.

Fourth, supposed evidence for reincarnation such as past-life recall (testimonies of past lives extracted through hypnotism) and cases of people knowing information impossible to obtain in their lifetime can be explained without recourse to reincarnation. Hypnotic evidence is far from certain. It has been found that people will sometimes report events that never happened; the subconscious is not an infallible guide. A leading New Age newsletter *The Brain-Mind Bulletin* reported that false memories induced by hypnotism "could limit the value of hypnosis in police investigations" according to a study conducted in Montreal.[60] Some supposed instances of memories from previous lives can also be regarded as cases of demon possession, in which supernaturally given information is used for deceptive purposes.[61]

Christ taught redemption, not reincarnation. Reconciliation to a holy and just God can happen but one way: through the redeeming work of Jesus Christ who invaded history to disclose the glory and love of God. Without ceasing to be God, Christ became a man to set us right with God. In doing this he claimed unique power and identity. He came not as one of many revelations ("avatars" in Hinduism) of the impersonal absolute, but as the personal revelation of the personal God. As the apostle John put it, "The Word [Christ] became flesh and lived for a while among us. We have seen his glory, the glory of the one and only Son, who came from the Father, full of grace and truth" (Jn 1:14). John, apostle of Jesus Christ, proclaimed Jesus as "the *only* Son."

The Gospels record Jesus not as a man who attained "Christ consciousness," but as the incarnate Savior and Lord. As John Stott summarizes: to know him was to know God (Jn 8:19; 14:7); to see him was to see God (Jn 12:45; 14:9); to believe in him was to believe in God (Jn 12:44; 14:1); to receive him was to receive God (Mk 9:37); to hate him was to hate God (Jn 15:23); to honor him was to honor God (Jn 5:23).[62] This controversial Jew, who trudged the streets of ancient Israel, who befriended the despised, who gathered to himself disciples of no fame or fortune, who performed miracles of healing and increase of food, who railed against the religious hypocrisy of his day, this prophet put to death for his convictions as were the prophets of old, claimed to be no less than God in the flesh. Unlike the "Gnostic Christ," he taught not as an illuminator of the One within, but as the Savior. He preached, "I am the way and the truth and the life. No one comes to the Father except through me" (Jn 14:6). And also, "I am the gate; whoever enters through me will be saved" (Jn 10:9).

Christ did not preach against the illusion of the separate ego; neither did he preach the divine within. Rather, he saw the human predicament as defined by sin, the willful transgression of God's standard. Out of the heart, he said, came uncleanness, not divinity (Mk 7:20–23). Christ taught that redemption comes through the forgiveness of sin, and he claimed the authority to do so. Christ offered himself not as an example of "Christ consciousness" but as a sacrifice for sin. As the apostle Paul put it, "God made him [Christ] who had no sin to be sin for us, so that in him we might become the righteousness of God" (2 Cor 5:21).

## Beyond Good and Evil?
A young woman in a New Age group once told me that if you were

"totally in the present"—by which she meant you had realized your own divinity—you could do anything, even rob a bank, and it would be all right. I asked her what she would think if it were her money that the "enlightened" one had stolen. But before she could answer I anticipated her reply: if you too were "totally in the present," it wouldn't matter. Though few would go to this extreme, it is logically consistent with the ideas that all is one, all is god and we are beyond good and evil.

Few people realize that Charles Manson was deeply immersed in the One for all. His involvement in several pantheistic groups (Scientology and others), plus his reading of occult materials while in prison, led him to believe that he had reached a state of consciousness beyond morality. He was free to kill, since killing is part of the One. R. C. Zaehner documents this in his book *Our Savage God* and says, "Charles Manson was absolutely sane: he had been *there,* where there is neither good nor evil."[63] The act of orchestrating and ordering the ritual murders of actress Sharon Tate and several others by his disciples was consistent with this understanding. Zaehner ponders:

> This is a great mystery—and the eternal paradox with which Eastern religions perpetually wrestle. If the ultimate truth, or the "perennial philosophy" as Aldous Huxley called it, is that "All is One" and "One is All," and that in this One all the opposites, including good and evil, are eternally reconciled, then have we any right to blame Charles Manson? For seen from the point of view of the eternal Now, he *did* nothing at all.[64]

Zaehner believes that Manson's atrocities were not insane but logical, given Manson's monistic viewpoint. Because he believed in the One, "many a 'rich pig' was to meet a gruesome and untimely end. . . . Charlie, so far from being mad had a lucidly logical mind."[65] According to an acquaintance, Manson "believed you could do no wrong, no bad. Everything was good. Whatever you do, you are following your own Karma."[66] A former follower of Manson explained that Manson would gain power over people by taking them on an LSD trip, telling them to give in to love and "how only by ceasing to exist as an individual ego could you become one with all things."[67] This reversibility of good and evil can also be seen by the fact that his followers knew him as both Satan and Christ.[68]

Few disciples of the One have the same agenda as this homicidal guru, but we should not dismiss his actions as those of an insane man or of a man who had no control of himself, a victim of sickness. In the philosophy of the One ethical distinctions evaporate; supposed opposites—light and dark, good and evil, humans and God—merge and fuse.

This example is not a lone eccentricity; history gives us another such gruesome lesson. The word *thug* originally referred to a class of religious assassins in northern India who terrorized the country for several hundred years before British pressure helped end their exploits. The thugs worshiped the Hindu goddess Kali, the wife of Shiva, a leading Hindu deity. She was, as noted earlier, a goddess of destruction and portrayed as smeared with blood, wearing a garland of human heads and chewing raw flesh.[69] In their dedication to Kali, the thugs ("deceivers") would go to great lengths of deception to ambush and strangle victims. As masters of their craft, they ritually sacrificed untold scores of people. Before the British crackdown in the 1830s approximately ten thousand thugs were at work. They destroyed life for their destroyer goddess. Nigel Davies helps the perplexed Westerner understand this bloodbath. We must detach ourselves from the Western, Christian idea that "God is love and the Devil is the enemy"[70] in order to understand that for the Hindu:

> God is both good and bad. . . . Man does not have to try to be good, but is perfectly free to copy either side of God's nature. The Hindu ascetic may aim at passive withdrawal from the world; but the Christian ideal of following in Jesus' footsteps of actively loving one's neighbor as oneself loses its point. If anything, the cruel side of the gods was easier to copy and the results more spectacular. Why should anyone have qualms about killing a fellow human

being in a colorful ceremony, when the great Shiva himself and his wife Kali delighted in destruction, bore in their hands the instruments of death, and fed on human flesh?[71]

This aspect of pantheism is seldom mentioned in New Age literature. Few in the movement would praise the monistic heritage of Kali, thugs and Manson. Yet they would essentially agree with the world view these groups held. Marilyn Ferguson shies away from talk about the historical consequences of the New Age world view, preferring to naively cling to an optimistic hope that the New Age will solve all ills. Yet we cannot ignore how this world view has proved itself in the past.

In discussing Hinduism, the Hindu scholar Coomarswamy tells us that one who realizes the real Self "no longer loves himself or others, but is the Self in himself and them." This person is not altruistic (having love *for the other*) but "literally un-self-ish," going beyond the self to the Self.[72]

The New Age lacks adequate criteria for judging human sin; it simply overlooks the existence of sin as a reality antithetical to righteousness. The distinction between good and evil is blurred, and the two become one. But as Christians we believe that God defines what is righteous and what is sinful according to his character and will. God is not "beyond good and evil" or "both good and evil." Morality is not an illusion generated from a retarded consciousness; it is a theological fact. God's moral character and commands are revealed both in the hearts of his creatures and in his written Word, the Bible. God is, in fact, the source of all good. To those who think otherwise he says through his prophet Isaiah, "Woe to those who call evil good and good evil, who put darkness for light and light for darkness" (Is 5:20). His way is life; rebellion against him means death. The God of the Bible has little in common with the One. Ethical discrimination is a crown of godliness and maturity for those Christians who "have trained themselves to distinguish good from evil" (Heb 5:14). Yet it is just this distinction that the One destroys.

## A Knowable God

The Christian God is rational and knowable. God speaks and God hears; he can be known as Father, Lord, Savior and friend. We cannot completely understand him, for there is mystery to the Godhead; but we may know him intellectually, spiritually, rationally and experientially.

Yet for New Age spirituality the experience of God-consciousness is beyond the personal and rational. Words themselves are often considered inadequate or inappropriate to use in speaking of oneness with the One. While not all New Age writers or practices negate the normal intellect, they usually seek to transcend it in the One.

To this the Christian responds by questioning the very logic of the assertion that God is beyond logical knowing. Even Rajneesh's statement that words cannot communicate truth precisely uses words to (try to) communicate truth. It is thus self-contradictory. If New Age seekers are to use religious experience as evidence for the truth of the One—as they often do—there must be a rational, conceptual component to the evidence, thus lending proof to something that can be spoken of logically. If an experience is "beyond rationality," how can it be used as a rational justification to believe that "all is one"?[73] In this sense, if the One is beyond logic and language, it is beyond belief. Carl Henry points this out:

> The insistence that the self is totally absorbed into the religious infinite, in an ecstatic union that transcends subject-object distinctions, would . . . seem to cancel out the mystic's ability to give a personal report of the actual state of things. For lapse of self-consciousness can only mean the surrender of any personal knowledge whatsoever.[74]

## An Exclusive God

New Age spirituality feels the pulse of the One at the spiritual heart of all religions, after the differing external trappings are peeled away. Yet if a unity of religions is not found in their stated creeds, the various religions must either be redefined according to another alien theology or an "esoteric core" superimposed on the religions, thus annulling their distinctive teachings. Paul Weiss has said that the "very stress on some common truth to be found in all [the religions], involves a dismissal of the distinctive affirmations of each. Actual religions are given up, then, for a philosophic category, an idle universal."[75]

We have seen that reconciliation between Christ and the One is impossible. We are faced not with a "both/and" but with an "either/ or." While "a niche has always been offered to Christ in 'the world's *pantheon*' . . . he claims the Throne."[76] Yet Christ's exclusiveness issues forth a call to all people to come to him for life. Christ warned of a wide road that leads to destruction and spoke of a narrow road leading to life (Mt 7:13-14). As P. T. Forsyth put it, "A gospel which is not exclusive will never include the world, for it will never master it. No religion will include devotees which does not exclude rivals."[77] The gospel of Christ is not a religious imperialism but a universal call to hope and faith. Jesus commissioned his disciples to disciple the nations and to preach his good news to all peoples (Mt 28:18-20). He will not share his glory with a raft of gurus, swamis, avatars or assorted holy men; neither will he cater to the wishes of neo-pagans, occultists or pantheistic mystics. Instead, he calls all to himself. He claims to be the one Savior and Lord.

Jesus warned of a multitude of impostors (Mt 24:24). While some truth can be found in nearly all religions, the truth of salvation is found only in Christ. The One gathers many religions into its hand, but the One cannot absorb the one who humbled himself to die on the cross for sin; this one has been exalted and given "the name that is above every name, that at the name of Jesus every knee should bow . . . and every tongue confess that Jesus Christ is Lord, to the glory of God the Father" (Phil 2:9-11).

# Challenging
# the One for All

## 8

As we've seen in these pages, the New Age is mounting an assault on Western culture. It believes its time has come. In this chapter we will explore further how the New Age is being packaged for modern tastes; then we will summarize the inherent flaws of the world view and the specific points at which Christianity parts ways with the New Age. We will also examine areas in which the New Age has influenced Christianity itself and what alternatives Christians can provide to counter the challenge of the New Age movement.

### Marketing the New Age

The New Age thrust can be divided into two categories: mainstream New Age and occult New Age. Earlier we defined the *occult* as any philosophy that seeks liberation from within the self by discovering the secret or hidden wisdom (gnosis); it may utilize a variety of practices: meditation, yoga, sensory deprivation, spirit-contact or others. In this sense the entire New Age movement is occult.

But in another sense, *occult* refers to exotic spiritual beliefs and practices such as mediumship, divination (crystal gazing, palmistry, tarot card reading, astrology) and the miraculous in general. American occultism, for example, is represented by groups such as the Theosophical Society. Occult books are usually published by small, obscure publishers and receive little attention. While such groups are no strangers in the West, their appeal is limited because of their "weird" reputation. Obvious occultism is simply not palatable to many moderns. But the New Age has another tack.

By "mainstream New Age" I mean that aspect of New Age thinking that packages its occult philosophy in culturally attractive and appealing wrappings. It enlists the respectability of science, psychology, medicine and established culture in general to further its appeal. For example, many scientifically oriented people may be won to Taoism or the New Age through Capra's *The Tao of Physics* than would be attracted to a book on Taoist meditation. The New Age must scratch where the culture itches. It must use the culture's language and whet its appetite for more.

David Spangler is a good example. He has spoken and written on the New Age for many years. His influence at Findhorn and his many books have left their mark. But his early books were published by Findhorn and not by a major publisher. For the uninitiated disciple, they were difficult to penetrate, being filled with the unique terminology and perplexing esotericism garnished from Theosophy and Alice Bailey's writings. Spangler spoke of occult doctrines such as the "Luciferic initiation."

But his approach has changed. Spangler's *Emergence: The Rebirth of the Sacred* (1984) is published by Doubleday and written for a general audience. His ideas have not changed, but they are more popularly available and attractive. Talk of Luciferic initiations and other occult rites are now gone, but the One for all is not.

Ferguson's *Aquarian Conspiracy* and Capra's *The Turning Point* similarly appeal to a broad audience and supply much more of an intellectual arsenal than Spangler. They are on the cultural cutting edge. And, as we have seen, they are essentially occult in their world view. They have merely translated occult terminology into the vernacular.

Many corporations are offering seminars and programs for the development of productivity, creativity and team spirit which incorporate New Age concepts. The Pacific Institute, a Seattle-based motivational training corporation, has offered its seminar "New Age Thinking" to scores of corporations, businesses and other groups including American Telephone and Telegraph, General Motors, the Internal Revenue Service, The Central Intelligence Agency, The United States Army, Navy and Air Force, and many police and fire departments.[1] The seminar emphasizes personal potential through affirmation and transformation. Warren Bennis, a management professor at the University of Southern California, says that as high as twenty per cent of the Fortune 500 corporations devote part of their budget for such "growth seminars."[2]

Just as the New Age movement must translate traditional occultism into culturally acceptable terms to bolster its attractiveness, so must it seek apologetic assistance from certain aspects of secular humanism—the waning but predominant world view of the West. As previously noted, the New Age and secular humanism are branches of the same tree. They both look to humanity for hope and salvation. They both reject the Christian God in favor of their own autonomous agenda. But the New Age's appeal lies in its mystical dimension. Humanism it remains, but a *cosmic* humanism; it is not content to treasure humanity's reason and technological prowess (like the old secular humanism) but instead emphasizes infinite human potential.

To increase its momentum and reach cultural ascendancy, the new cosmic humanism must integrate its religious orientation with rational conviction. As Marxism labors to do to this day, it must fuse transcendent yearnings with intellectual passion. Only by incorporating the benefits and advances of scientific humanism will the New Age be able to get the modern world to listen.

But this venture is ultimately doomed. Despite its promise of a New Age of unlimited human potential, the movement finds itself impaled by its own world view. Ultimately it is unable to forge a credible synthesis between the spiritual and rational. We see this clearly in three areas.

## The Reality of Finiteness

Although the appeal to the divinity of humanity has a perennial allure, humanity has never been up for the task. Just as secular humanism exhausts and sabotages its own resources by limiting truth to the unaided human understanding, so the New Age also runs aground on the hard reality of our finitude and imperfection. The appeal to our infinite potential caters more to pride than reality. All human experience is necessarily bracketed by our creaturely limitations.

Secular humanism's desacralized universe edited out the supernatural and left a world bereft of transcendence. Cosmic humanism overcompensates by reinvesting the world and people with a counterfeit significance discovered through the oneness of all things. The New Age tries to erase the realities of time, space, mortality and individuality.

Even a small sampling of human experience and history reveals a humanity in need of external support. Besides our created limitations as finite, dependent beings, the ravages of a defiled conscience, the inescapability of death and the fact of our inhumanity to each other all point to the impossibility of self-salvation. As Gary North comments:

> Those who have sought power and meaning apart from God have at times found power, both rational and occult, but the ultimate hope—that there is meaning in the world apart from that imposed on creation by a sovereign personal God—cannot be achieved.

Power does not satisfy and meaning does not stem from man, the hypothetical measure of all things.[3]

## The Problem of Goodness

The New Age world view ultimately dissolves moral distinctions and plunges itself into moral ambiguity, if not anarchy. As mentioned before, the idea of the oneness of all things demands the erasing of all distinctions and dualities. The division between good and evil is abolished. While this conclusion is not always clearly stated in New Age writings, it flows logically from the world view.

The new cosmic humanism, then, is as relativistic ethically as the older secular humanism. Not only is "man the measure of all things," as the humanistic saying goes, but "man is all things" and the creator of all reality. The New Age aspirant differs little from Nietzsche's "Superman"—the one who overcomes the old view of humanity by "transvaluating" all values according to his own whim, going "beyond good and evil."

But no world view can consistently deny ethical realities. The New Age has an agenda and a philosophy. It views those who oppose it as wrong, absolutely wrong. When Ferguson lays out a chart comparing the "old paradigm" with the "new paradigm," she clearly favors the new and disregards the old, despite her claim to transcend either/or logic.[4] By its own logic the New Age has no basis for saying that it is good or even true. These categories cannot exist.

## The Loss of Objectivity

The New Age thus suffers from a crisis of knowing (epistemology). While it claims a universal and unified world view, the New Age cannot adequately anchor that world view in objective reality. Instead it appeals to human subjectivity—the divine within—as its prime source of truth. The idea of an objective revelation from a higher, divine authority is replaced by the search within.[5] Accordingly, the subconscious realm of dream, fantasy and all manner of subjective experiences are given free rein as the distiller of revelation and truth.

But human consciousness is too ambiguous and unpredictable to serve as the basis for a world view. Modern psychology has shown the human proneness to illusion, deception and vanity.[6] A prophet long ago said that the heart was "desperately wicked" such that no one could even understand it (Jer 17:9). As Chesterton said, "One may understand the cosmos, but never the ego; the self is more distant than any star. Thou shalt love the Lord thy God; but thou shalt not know thyself."[7] The subterranean depths of the psyche are littered with too many horrific hazards to be safely navigated apart from a more stable reference point.

This subjective epistemology easily slips into subjectivism and solipsism. Each person has their own "space" or beliefs which may be held with little or no rational justification. In his book *The New Nonsense,* Charles Fair sees us as "entering an era of willful personal belief," which, in the short run, simplifies our beliefs. He says that "not only do we feel free to live according to any set of values we choose; there is no need for them to make any ultimate sense. The important thing is for us to *like* them, for them to give us good 'vibes.' "[8] For every person there is a different reality. A unified world view is not possible.

## The Dynamics of Deception

Just how can this experience of oneness and infinite potential, which is so real and powerful to many, be explained without embracing the One for all? Experiences of divinity and oneness may be explained naturally or supernaturally. Some have argued that the mental states reached through meditation are not higher states of consciousness, but are actually lower than normal consciousness. The ability to differentiate between concepts and objects is reduced to the point of a blanket homogeneity of being.[9] It is also possible that some experiences of oneness reflect the reality of God's unifying work in creation, but become deceptive when the experience stops at the level of the creation and does not go on and praise God the Creator for his works (Rom 1:21).

The experience of "one primal being unconfronted by another" was not unfamiliar to the Jewish philosopher, Martin Buber.[10] From his own "unforgettable experience" Buber sought to understand a "state in which the bonds of the personal nature of life seem to [fall] away from us [and] we experience an undivided unity."[11] But Buber's Jewish theological commitment to the inescapable I–Thou relationship between man and God prompted him to avoid the One. He interpreted the experience as revealing the unity of his own soul, but not the soul (the One) of all. Buber viewed his soul as "existing but once, single, unique, irreplaceable, this creaturely one; one of the human souls and not the 'soul of the All': a defined and particular being and not 'Being.' "[12] Buber assessed his experience as being beneath the joy and responsibility of dialog (the meeting of two individuals), not above it, as being farther from God and not nearer to him. Buber met the One and called it a liar.

Other experiences may be directly demonic, resulting from an altered state of consciousness that leaves one open to malevolent spiritual manipulation. In general, an experience *per se* does not guarantee its truth. The apostle John, thoroughly familiar with spiritual counterfeits, warned us to "test the spirits to see whether they are from God" (1 Jn 4:1).

## Christian Essentials

The New Age challenges the modern mindset on a variety of fronts. As we have seen, it is not always clear what parts of the New Age are corrective and what parts are harmful. Ultimately these issues come down to a clash of world views. As Christians we must reject any practice or belief that contradicts our faith. Throughout the ages, Christianity has been attacked on all sides. Secular humanism called it superstitious and supernatural. The New Age often identifies it with Western rationalism and scientism. But Christianity must be encountered as it is, not as it has been caricatured. I have summarized below the essentials of a Christian world view which we must keep in mind as we confront the New Age. (Also I have provided a chart that compares the secular humanist, New Age and Christian world views.)

*1. Personal.* The Christian world view could be summarized as *cosmic personalism.*[13] The cosmos and all it contains must be understood according to its personal and sovereign Creator. God is the creator and ground of our personality as creatures; we are made in God's personal image (Gen 1:26) as his special creatures. Human personality is a gift of God—not a hindrance to enlightenment.

Because of the distinction between God the Creator and the universe as his creation, people must relate to God in what Martin Buber called an "I-Thou" relationship. Christianity rejoices in the uniqueness of individuals and the relationships between them. Speaking to this issue, G. K. Chesterton challenged Theosophist Annie Besant's notion of "the universal self." After saying that she "does not tell us to love our neighbors; she tells us to be our neighbors," Chesterton says:

> I want to love my neighbor not because he is I, but precisely because he is not I. I want to adore the world, not as one likes a looking-glass, because it is one's self, but as one loves a woman, because she is entirely different. If souls are separate, love is possible. If souls are united love is obviously impossible. . . . If the world is full of real selves, they can be really unselfish selves. But upon Mrs. Besant's principle the whole cosmos is only one enormously selfish person.[14]

Christianity rejects egotism, not the ego itself. The self must stay, but not selfishness. The self must serve the holy God.

*2. Supernatural.* While the spiritual world interpenetrates the natural world it is not identical with it. God is transcendent—above his creation; he is *super*natural. He is free to miraculously intervene in the normal workings of his creation when he deems fit, as the Bible amply demonstrates. Christ's resurrection from the dead is the greatest example. The Christian views God's miracles, then, as supernat-

## The Secular Humanist, New Age and Christian World Views

| | Secular Humanist | New Age | Christian |
|---|---|---|---|
| **1. Metaphysics** God and the world | Universe is self-existent, no God | God is the world, pantheism | Creator/creation distinction |
| Nature of God | God is a superstition | God is impersonal/amoral | God is personal/moral |
| Nature of world *(cosmology)* | Matter/energy, atomistic | All is spirit/consciousness, monistic | Creation of God upheld by God, interconnected but not monistic |
| **2. Epistemology** *(basis for knowledge)* | Man is measure of all things, reason and science | Man is all things, truth within | Truth revealed in the Bible |
| **3. Ethics** | Autonomous and situational (relative) | Autonomous and situational (relative) | Based on the revelation of God's will, absolute |
| **4. Nature of Humans** | Evolved animal | Spiritual being, a sleeping God | Made in the image of God, now fallen |
| **5. Human Problem** | Superstition, ignorance | Ignorance of true potential | Sin—rebellion against God and his law |
| **6. Answer to Human Problems** | Reason and technology | Change of consciousness | Faith in and obedience to Christ |
| **7. History** | Linear but chance | Cyclical | Linear and providential |
| **8. Death** | End of existence | Illusion, entrance to next life (reincarnation) | Entrance to either eternal heaven or hell |
| **9. View of Religion** | Superstition, some good moral teaching | All point to the One (syncretism) | Not all from God, teach different things |
| **10. View of Jesus Christ** | Moral teacher | One of many avatars (periodic manifestations of God-guru) | The unique God-Man, only Lord and Savior |

urally caused. Demonic manifestations are likewise caused by the spiritual world interfering with the material world (although the New Age equates the supernatural to innate human abilities). The New Age view of the miraculous should be called *para*natural, not supernatural, because it sees nothing "above" nature. Unlike the New Age follower, the Christian seeks help "from above," not "from within." The Christian seeks to know the power and presence of the supernatural God.

*3. Ethical.* The Bible declares that God is holy and morally perfect. According to Donald Bloesch, "in biblical faith . . . God signifies a purity of love that excludes and judges evil. The true God is neither beyond good and evil nor does he encompass good and evil, but he is the perfect good that negates evil and sets it off as an antithesis to his holy will."[15]

This was burned into the prophet Isaiah's experience when he saw God "seated on a throne, high and exalted" (Is 6:1). Above God Isaiah saw seraphs (heavenly beings) "calling to one another: 'Holy, holy, holy is the LORD Almighty' " (v. 3), whereupon the temple Isaiah was in began to shake and be filled with smoke. Overcome by the holiness of God, he exclaimed, "Woe to me. . . . I am ruined! For I am a man of unclean lips, and I live among a people of unclean lips, and my eyes have seen the King, the LORD Almighty" (v. 5). A seraph then touched Isaiah's lips with a hot coal and announced that his guilt was taken away and his sin atoned for (v. 7). Only then was Isaiah ready for his prophetic mission.

*4. Rational.* Christian faith avoids both the rationalism of secular humanism and the irrational tendencies of New Age subjectivism. While it asserts that God's truth is not the result of human thought, it does not denounce reason but sees it as a God-given capacity and an indication of our being created in the image of a rational God (Gen 1:26-28; Jn 1:1-3, 9). Yet human reason is now affected by sin and misdirected such that God's wisdom appears foolish to unredeemed people (1 Cor 2)—not because it is illogical in itself, but because the pride of humanity balks at a gospel that convicts the world of its utter inability to save itself. God's revelation in the Bible is reasonably presented and approachable to all who humbly inquire of it. Paul's epistle to the Romans, for example, is a detailed, logical treatise on the essentials of Christian faith.

*5. Experiential.* The Christian understanding of reason does not deny or downplay the importance of experience. God is Lord of the whole person—reason, emotion, will, imagination. Personal experiences of God's love and grace saturate the Bible. The fruit of the Holy Spirit's work in the Christian life include love, joy and peace (Gal 5:22)—all subjective experiences. Christianity touches the heart without by-passing the mind; Christians are called to love the Lord with all their heart, soul, strength and mind. In fact, the Bible does not separate heart and mind, but sees them as a unity.

Christians, then, have nothing to fear from recent studies, often alluded to in New Age materials, indicating two different kinds of knowing corresponding to the right and left hemispheres of the brain. Although the research is just beginning and simplifications are dangerous, findings show that the right hemisphere is primarily concerned with intuitive experience and seeing wholes or patterns, while the left hemisphere embraces the more verbal, abstract and logical dimensions. The Bible itself addresses both ways of knowing in the diversity of its literature. Whether it be Paul's detailed theology, the Mosaic Law, David's psalms, or the visions given to Ezekiel, John and others, the Bible offers us a full-orbed revelation embracing the whole person.[16]

*6. Holistic.* Since God is the Lord and Owner of the entire created universe, Christianity covers the whole of life; it is holistic, understanding all things in relation to each other and in relation to God. The creation is an interrelated whole orchestrated by the plan and power of God. Nothing is beyond his providential care and control. Neither can the creation be viewed in isolation from humanity. Both are bound together. The God of the Bible declares that our moral actions influence the earth; the breaking of God's covenant resulted in ecological as well as ethical desolation (Ps 107:33-38; Is 24:1-6; Hos 4:1-3).

*7. Objective.* Along with being holistic, Christianity is also objective, providing a standard beyond and above the created world by which to evaluate all of life. Truth is not based on subjective experience but on God's revelation of himself in the Bible and through Christ.

While the New Age world view seeks to be holistic, it has no objective grounding because it has no personal and morally perfect God that transcends the creation. Truth itself becomes nebulous for the New Age—lost in subjective "space" and the "multiple realities"—as do moral distinctions between good and evil. Yet the God of the Bible has given us an objective operating manual for the planet, that we may be equipped to obey him in every area of life and thought (2 Tim 3:16).

*8. Historical.* Unlike much of New Age thought, Christianity views history as linear, not cyclical. New Age views of history often take their cue from Eastern religions, which see history as a repetition of endless cycles or ages. Just as people are reincarnated, so civilizations are born and reborn endlessly without final judgment. Biblically, history flows according to the command of God; it has a beginning (creation), a middle (incarnation) and an end (the second coming of Christ). History is charged with an anticipatory significance and is to be redeemed for the glory of God. It is not perpetual repetition but the theater of human action in which people and nations either obey God and are blessed, or disobey him and are cursed (Deut 8, 28; Jer 18:5-10).

## Compromises

Just as the New Age has infiltrated many disciplines with the attractiveness of its views, it has also seduced some Christians. Ignorance of sound doctrine leaves the church spiritually ill-equipped to resist deception. Unfortunately, some have compromised Christianity by assimilating New Age ideas and practices. This is particularly true in some areas of Christian teaching.

First, an imbalanced emphasis is sometimes placed on subjective introspection. The Christian faith is mixed with certain psychological theories and practices—such as Jungian therapy—which emphasize excavating and interpreting the inner recesses of the mind. Although our sanctification should embrace the whole person and reach into the caverns of the psychological deep, we must be careful to set our course by Christ. Because of indwelling sin, the "journey inward" must be courted with great caution and, in many cases, simply avoided. Although Christians are justified by faith through grace and are delivered from the penalty of sin, our sanctification is not complete until the world to come. Unlike New Age philosophy, Christianity teaches that corruption, not salvation, comes from within. We need to look beyond ourselves to become better selves. As Paul said, "Since, then, you have been raised with Christ, set your hearts on things above, where Christ is seated at the right hand of God. Set your minds on things above, not on earthly things" (Col 3:1-2). The subconscious should not be viewed as a pure channel of revelation; rather, God's Word must direct our thoughts and life.

Second, Christians should be careful when considering Christian mystical writings. Although biblical Christians have recorded their personal encounters with God for our benefit, many mystics even within the general Christian tradition have taught things that oppose Christian doctrine. This is especially the case with those who speak of their personalities being absorbed in the divine. Some Christian mystics are, in fact, lauded by the New Age. These are, by and large, those mystics who show affinity with pantheistic monism.[17]

Even some contemporary Christian writings stress the believer's "union with Christ" so as to border on pantheism. We are, indeed, made in the divine image and resemble God in a finite fashion. Peter could say of Christians that we "participate in the divine nature"

(2 Pet 1:4); but, as Abraham Kuyper pointed out, "according to all sound expositors, this means only that unto the sinner are imparted the attributes of goodness and holiness, which he originally possessed in his own nature in common with the divine nature, but which was lost by sin. . . . But this may not be understood as obliterating the boundary between the divine nature and the human."[18] Salvation is not deification; redeemed humanity should never be confused with divinity.[19]

Third, in some Christian circles an unhealthy emphasis is placed on positive thinking or positive confession—the idea being that whatever we believe or verbally affirm will become a reality. Although it is a mark of vibrant faith to maintain a biblical optimism in the face of obstacles, an overemphasis on positive thinking may come perilously close to the New Age idea that thought controls reality and that we are masters of the world. This view overlooks the mystery of God's providence, his final control of all events. God answers prayer and has given us authority for spiritual conflict (see Eph 6), but we don't have God on a string; neither can we as fallen and finite creatures expect reality to jump at our command. Faith is not magic. We should not affirm "mind over matter," but God's sovereignty over his creation.[20]

Fourth, some Christians' interest in ecology leads them into New Age territory. Some Christians, concerned about severe ecological problems, claim that the "creation mandate" of Genesis 1:28-30 has been annulled and that we must closely identify the creation with the Creator by downplaying God's transcendence over creation. Yet the creation mandate was never annulled (see Gen 9:1-3 and Ps 8). As stewards we are to exercise a lawful dominion over creation for the glory of God. Although humans are of more value than the animal kingdom to God (Mt 6:26), this in no way demeans ecological stewardship. We must affirm both the transcendence and immanence of God, being careful to resist a pantheistic romanticizing of creation. The creation is not an emanation of God; rather it is his good world made from nothing *(ex nihilo)* and upheld by his constant providence.

To be discerning, we must avoid paranoia. Not every Christian who uses catch phrases or buzz words similar to those used by the New Age is somehow a part of it. Any individual Christian or Christian group should be evaluated according to all relevant considerations such as stated goals, doctrine and actual fruits. For instance, the terms *global* and *planetary* get much use by the New Age, but this does not mean that all who use the words are a part of the New Age. This would be guilt by semantic association—hardly a convincing verdict. Yet some have falsely condemned Christian groups and individuals on scanty evidence. What is needed is a positive Christian agenda to counter the claims and plans of the New Age.

## Witnessing to the New Age

All truth is God's truth, whether it be from the Bible or from the mouth of a New Age follower. Nevertheless, Christians must learn to witness to the truth of their faith and to expose the weaknesses of the New Age. Effectively confronting the New Age will take a humble, loving spirit and conscious effort at reaching out to those in the movement

We need to look for legitimate common ground with the New Age. We've noted that the New Age raises crucial issues for the modern world. This can be used as a springboard in communicating Christ to the New Age. We can agree on some things. As John Calvin noted about reading non-Christian authors:

The admirable light of truth displayed in them should remind us that the human mind, however much fallen and perverted from its original integrity, is still adorned with admirable gifts from the Creator. If we reflect that the Spirit of God is the only fountain of truth, we will be careful, as we would avoid offering insult to him, not to reject or condemn truth wherever it appears.[21]

At the same time we affirm the common ground between the New Age and Christianity we must clearly specify and define the differences between the world views. Because the New Age generally believes that all roads lead to God, Christians must clearly explain how

Christianity contradicts the One. But we cannot stop there. Christians must develop viable alternatives and convictions on subjects of special interest to the New Age. In short, the Christian response to the New Age involves three things: watching, evaluating and acting.

*Watching.* Christians should become culture watchers to discern the presence and influence of New Age ideas—that we might not be taken unaware. Areas of special concern are education and politics, both of which are often shielded by elitist insulation and popular apathy. Parents are frequently oblivious to public school curriculum as are most citizens to political affairs. Thus the One can enter and entice these areas with relative ease unless it is exposed by those alert to its charms.[22]

*Evaluating.* Chronicling error is not sufficient. False philosophies must be refuted, not just exposed. In this book I've tried to outline a Christian response to the New Age. I hope these principles will help when you encounter the One. Scripture tells us to both have a reason for our faith (1 Pet 3:16) and reasons against the New Age (2 Cor 10:3-5).

*Acting.* Christianity is a full-orbed world and life view. It cannot afford to emphasize only error; instead it must implement the truth into all areas of life and thought. If Christians abandon crucial aspects of culture—education, politics, science, psychology, health and others—counterfeit philosophies will naturally and militantly fill the void. Because this has happened in the recent past, Christians are partially responsible for the rise of the New Age. When and where Christians retreat, the enemy advances.

The new cosmic humanism of the New Age threatens to become the consensus. This should cause us to shudder in horror. The pantheistic consensus in India has perpetuated the country's poverty, misery and hopelessness for thousands of years. Any world view at odds with the truth of God and his creation can only wreak havoc wherever it plants roots.[23] "Unless the LORD builds the house, its builders labor in vain" (Ps 127:1).

As a faithful Christian community dedicated to loving God and neighbor, we must attempt to reverse this trend and make a difference in the world. Donning the armor and weapons of the Spirit (Eph 6:10-18) and equipped with a full-orbed Christian world view (Rom 12:1-2), we must try to prayerfully and actively stem the tide of the One for all.

# Notes

**Chapter One: The One for All**

[1]Francis Adeney, "Educators Look East," *Spiritual Counterfeits Journal* 5, no. 1 (Winter 1981), p. 28.

[2]Ibid., p. 29.

[3]Ibid.

[4]Shirley MacLaine, *Out on a Limb* (Toronto: Bantam, 1983), p. 351.

[5]Ibid., p. 352.

[6]Erich Fromm, *To Have or to Be?* (New York: Harper and Row, 1976), p. 125.

[7]Ibid. Fromm's italics.

[8]Ibid.

[9]Ibid., p. 127.

[10]James Sire, *The Universe Next Door* (Downers Grove, Ill.: InterVarsity Press, 1976), p. 17.

[11]Ayn Rand, *Romantic Manifesto* (New York: New American Library, 1975), p. 19.

[12]Jeremy Rifkin, *Entropy: A New World View* (New York: Viking Press, 1980), p. 5.

[13]Lewis Mumford, *The Transformations of Man* (New York: Harper and Row, 1972), p. 179.

[14]Fritjof Capra, *The Turning Point* (New York: Simon and Schuster, 1982), p. 371.

[15]C. S. Lewis, *Miracles* (New York: Macmillan, 1947), p. 169.

[16]C. S. Lewis, *The Problem of Pain* (New York: Macmillan, 1962), pp. 150-51.

[17]Lancelot Law Whyte, *The Universe of Experience* (New York: Harper and Row, 1974), p. 6.

[18]Paul Williams, *Das Energy* (New York: Warner, 1973), p. 129.

[19]Theodore Roszak, *Unfinished Animal* (New York: Harper and Row, 1977), p. 225.

[20]Quoted in Dave Hunt, *The Cult Explosion* (Irvine, Calif.: Harvest House, 1980), p. 106.

[21]Quoted in Dave Hunt, *Peace, Prosperity, and the Coming Holocaust* (Eugene, Oreg.: Harvest House, 1983), p. 82.

[22]George Leonard, *The Silent Pulse* (New York: Bantam, 1981), p. 105.

[23]Michael Murphy and Rhea A. White, *The Psychic Side of Sports* (Reading, Mass.: Addison-Wesley, 1978), pp. 5-6.

[24]Ibid., pp. 142-50.

[25]Ibid., pp. xx.

[26]Ibid., p. 109.

[27]Fritjof Capra, *The Tao of Physics* (Boulder, Colo.: Shambhala, 1975), p. 11.

[28]John Weldon, "est," in *A Guide to Cults and New Religions*, ed. Ronald Enroth (Downers Grove, Ill.: InterVarsity Press, 1983), p. 81.

[29]Ibid., p. 76.

[30]George Leonard, "The End of Sex," *Esquire*, December 1982, p. 80.

[31]Alan Vaughan, "Intuition, Precognition, and the Art of Prediction," *The Futurist*, June 1982, p. 10.

[32]William Goldstein, "Life on the Astral Plane," *Publishers Weekly*, 18 March 1983, p. 46.

[33]Bhagwan Shree Rajneesh, *I Am the Gate* (New York: Harper and Row, 1977), p. 18.

[34]James M. Robinson, ed., *The Nag Hammadi Library* (San Francisco: Harper and Row, 1981), p. 126.

[35]Julian Huxley, *Religion without Revelation* (London: Max Parrish, 1959), p. 236.

[36]William Irwin Thompson, *From Nation to Emanation* (Scotland: Findhorn Publications, 1982), p. 52.

[37]George Leonard, *The Transformation* (New York: Delta, 1972), p. 2.

[38]Barbara Marx Hubbard, "The Future of Futurism," *The Futurist*, April 1983, p. 52.

[39]Ibid., p. 55.

[40]Ibid.

[41]Barbara Marx Hubbard, *The Evolutionary Journey* (San Francisco: Evolutionary Press, 1982), p. 157.

[42]Thompson, *From Nation to Emanation*, p. 13.

[43]Marilyn Ferguson, *The Aquarian Conspiracy* (Los Angeles: J. P. Tarcher, 1980), p. 25.

[44]Ibid., pp. 62-63.

[45]Ibid., p. 213.

[46]Ibid., p. 216.

[47]Ibid., p. 217.

[48]Hubbard, "The Future of Futurism," p. 56.

[49]Richard Hofstadter, *The Paranoid Style in American Politics* (New York: Alfred A. Knopf, 1965), p. 36.

[50]Ibid., p. 37.

[51]Ibid., pp. 37-38.

[52]For a critique of New Age conspiracy theories see Brooks Alexander, "The Final Threat: Apocalypse, Conspiracy, and Biblical Faith," *Spiritual Counterfeits Newsletter* 10, no. 1 (January/February 1984), pp. 1ff., and Eric Pement, "Consensus or Conspir-

acy," *Cornerstone* 11, no. 64, pp. 16ff.
⁵³Pement, "Consensus or Conspiracy," p. 35.

**Chapter Two: From the Counterculture to the New Age**
¹Ferguson, *Aquarian,* p. 89.
²Bertrand Russell, *Why I Am Not a Christian* (New York: Simon and Schuster, 1957), p. 107.
³See Sire, *Universe Next Door,* pp. 59-91, for an exposition of how naturalism (secular humanism) leads to nihilism.
⁴Theodore Roszak, *Where the Wasteland Ends* (Garden City, N.Y.: Doubleday, 1972), p. 123.
⁵Ibid., p. 132.
⁶Eric Hoffer, *The True Believer* (New York: Harper and Row, 1966), p. 119.
⁷Jerry Rubin, *Growing (Up) at Thirty-Seven* (New York: M. Evans, 1976), p. 199.
⁸See Elliot Miller, "The New Age Movement: What Is It?" *Forward* (Summer 1985), pp. 20-21.
⁹Ferguson, *Aquarian,* p. 68.
¹⁰Ibid., adapted from pp. 86-87.
¹¹Ibid., p. 87. For a critique of how fantasy games like Dungeons and Dragons may involve people in New Age ideas, see John Weldon and James Bjornstad, *Playing with Fire* (Chicago: Moody Press, 1984).
¹²Peter Berger, *The Heretical Imperative* (Garden City, N.Y.: Anchor, 1979), pp. 20-23.
¹³Ferguson, *Aquarian,* p. 45.
¹⁴C. S. Lewis, *Miracles,* pp. 82-83. For a history of pantheism see "The One in History," Douglas Groothuis (unpublished manuscript) and Rousas John Rushdoony, *The One and the Many* (Nutley, N.J.: Craig Press, 1971).
¹⁵Morris Berman, *The Reenchantment of the World* (Ithaca, N.Y.: Cornell University Press, 1981), p. 23.
¹⁶Hoffer, *True Believer,* p. 69.
¹⁷Ibid., p. 18.
¹⁸Peter Russell, *The Global Brain* (Los Angeles: J. P. Tarcher, 1983), p. 99.
¹⁹Hubbard, *Evolutionary Journey,* p. 44.
²⁰Ibid., p. 27.
²¹Ernst Cassirer, *The Philosophy of the Enlightenment* (Boston: Beacon Press, 1964), p. 41.
²²"What Is Humanism?" *Manas,* 30 January 1980, p. 2.
²³Cassirer, *Philosophy of the Enlightenment,* p. 138.
²⁴"What Is Humanism?" pp. 7-8.
²⁵Carl Sagan, *Cosmos* (New York: Random House, 1980), p. 4.
²⁶Paul Kurtz, ed., *Humanist Manifestos I and II* (Buffalo, N.Y.: Prometheus, 1979), p. 16.
²⁷Brooks Alexander, "The Rise of Cosmic Humanism: What Is Religion?" *Spiritual Counterfeits Journal* 5, no. 1 (Winter 1981), p. 2.
²⁸For an excellent critique of this viewpoint, see Carl F. H. Henry, *The Remaking of the Modern Mind* (Grand Rapids, Mich.: Eerdmans, 1948), pp. 119-71.
²⁹Quoted in Greg Bahnsen, "On Worshiping the Creature Rather Than the Creator," *The Journal of Christian Reconstruction* 1, no. 1 (Summer 1974), p. 114.

[30]Ibid.

[31]Keith Thompson, "Soviet Adventures in Consciousness," *New Age,* March 1982, p. 33.

[32]Ibid.

[33]Ibid., p. 35.

[34]C. S. Lewis, *The Screwtape Letters* (New York: Macmillan, 1961), p. 33.

[35]Kurtz, *Humanist Manifestos,* p. 16.

[36]Mircea Eliade, *Occultism, Witchcraft, and Cultural Fashions* (Chicago: University of Chicago Press, 1976), p. 5.

[37]Quoted in Alexander, "Rise of Cosmic Humanism," p. 5.

[38]Ibid., p. 6.

## Chapter Three: Holistic Health

[1]Quoted in Andrew Weil, *Health and Healing* (Boston: Houghton Mifflin, 1983), p. 111.

[2]Ferguson, *Aquarian,* p. 242.

[3]The following is greatly indebted to Paul C. Reisser, Teri K. Reisser and John Weldon, *The Holistic Healers* (Downers Grove, Ill.: InterVarsity Press, 1983), pp. 14-32.

[4]Capra, *Turning Point,* p. 123.

[5]Ibid., p. 134.

[6]Weil, *Health and Healing,* p. 51.

[7]Capra, *Turning Point,* p. 158.

[8]Ferguson, *Aquarian,* p. 248.

[9]Weil, *Health and Healing,* p. 37.

[10]Kerry Pechter, "Hands-on Health: An Illustrated Guide to the Manipulative Arts," *Prevention,* March 1984, p. 50.

[11]Larry Dossey, *Space, Time, and Medicine* (Boulder, Colo.: Shambhala, 1982).

[12]Reisser et al., *Holistic Healers,* p. 25.

[13]Ibid.

[14]Geraldine Youcha, "Psychiatrists and Folk Magic," *Science Digest,* June 1981, p. 50.

[15]Michael Harner, *The Way of the Shaman* (New York: Bantam, 1982), p. 175.

[16]Dio Urmella Neff, "Tantra: A Tradition Unveiled: Part 1," *Yoga Journal,* January/February 1983, p. 10.

[17]Leonard, "End of Sex," p. 80.

[18]Quoted in Brooks Alexander, "Holistic Health from the Inside," *Spiritual Counterfeits Journal,* August 1978, p. 10.

[19]Larry Dossey, "Space, Time, and Medicine," *Revision* 5, no. 2 (Fall 1982), p. 54.

[20]Reisser et al., *Holistic Healers,* p. 29.

[21]See ibid., pp. 33-49 for a developed view.

[22]Dossey, "Space, Time," p. 55. For a biblical reflection on the meaning of time see William T. McConnell, *The Gift of Time* (Downers Grove, Ill.: InterVarsity Press, 1983).

[23]Reisser et al., *Holistic Healers,* p. 31.

[24]Capra, *Turning Point,* pp. 333-34.

[25]Ferguson, *Aquarian,* pp. 259-60.

[26]Ivan Illich, *The Medical Nemesis* (New York: Pantheon, 1982), pp. 270-71.

[27]Ibid., p. 3.

[28]Reisser et al., *Holistic Healers,* p. 20.

[29]See ibid., pp. 53-62.

[30]G. K. Chesterton, *Saint Francis of Assisi* (Garden City, N.Y.: Image, 1957), p. 28.

[31]Clifford Wilson and John Weldon, *Occult Shock and Psychic Forces* (San Diego: Master, 1980), p. 182.

[32]See John Weldon and Zola Levitt, *Psychic Healing: An Exposé of an Occult Phenomenon* (Chicago: Moody Press, 1982), pp. 191-208.

[33]The Bible repeatedly condemns occult activity; see Ex 7:11-12; 22:18; Lev 19:26, 31; 20:6, 27; Zech 10:2; Mal 3:5; Acts 8:9; 16:16; 19:19; 1 Sam 28; 1 Chron 10:13-14; Is 2:6; 8:19; Jer 27:9-10; Gal 5:20; Rev 21:8; 22:15.

[34]D. Gareth Jones, *Our Fragile Brains* (Downers Grove, Ill.: InterVarsity Press, 1981), pp. 212-19; see also Wilson and Weldon, *Occult Shock*, pp. 221-26.

[35]For tools in evaluating practices see Reisser et al., *Holistic Healers*, pp. 122-32.

[36]Martin Bobgan and Deidre Bobgan, *Hypnosis and the Christian* (Minneapolis: Bethany House, 1984); and Hunt, *Peace, Prosperity*, pp. 111-23.

[37]See Wilson and Weldon, *Occult Shock*, pp. 71-78; and Kurt Koch, *The Devil's Alphabet* (Grand Rapids, Mich.: Kregel, 1971), pp. 123-27.

[38]See Reisser et al., *Holistic Healers*, pp. 63-78.

[39]Wilson and Weldon, *Occult Shock*, pp. 247-63, 273-84.

[40]Weill, *Health and Healing*, p. 182.

[41]S. I. McMillen, *None of These Diseases* (Old Tappan, N.J.: Revel, 1968).

[42]R. K. Harrison, quoted in Gerhard F. Hasel, "Health and Healing in the Old Testament," *Andrews University Seminary Studies* 21, no. 3 (Autumn 1983), p. 194.

[43]See David E. Allen, Lewis P. Bird, Robert Herrman, *Whole-Person Medicine* (Downers Grove, Ill.: InterVarsity Press, 1980); and Charles E. Hummel, *Fire in the Fireplace* (Downers Grove, Ill.: InterVarsity Press, 1978), pp. 207-23.

## Chapter Four: Exploring Human Potential in Psychology

[1]Martin Gross, *The Psychological Society* (New York: Simon and Schuster, 1978), p. 3.

[2]Ibid., p. 4.

[3]Peter Berger, Brigitte Berger, Hansfried Kellner, *The Homeless Mind* (New York: Random House, 1974), pp. 77-78.

[4]Quoted in Claudia Wallis, "Stress: Can We Cope?" *Time*, 6 June 1983, p. 48.

[5]Ibid.

[6]Quoted in Frank Goble, *The Third Force* (New York: Pocket Books, 1971), p. 5.

[7]See Martin Bobgan and Deidre Bobgan, *The Psychological Way/The Spiritual Way* (Minneapolis, Minn.: Bethany Fellowship, 1979), pp. 68-85; and Rousas John Rushdoony, *Freud* (Phillipsburg, N.J.: Presbyterian and Reformed, 1978), for Christian critiques of Freud.

[8]Quoted in Bobgan and Bobgan, *Psychological Way/Spiritual Way*, p. 76.

[9]Gross, *Psychological Society*, pp. 18-54.

[10]Viktor Frankl, *Man's Search for Meaning* (New York: Pocket Books, 1973).

[11]Quoted in Viktor Frankl, *The Unheard Cry for Meaning* (New York: Simon and Schuster, 1978), p. 28.

[12]Viktor Frankl, *The Unconscious God* (New York: Simon and Schuster, 1975), p. 93.

[13]See David Erhenfeld, *The Arrogance of Humanism* (New York: Oxford University Press, 1978), pp. 80-81.

[14]Abraham H. Maslow, *Toward a Psychology of Being* (New York: Van Nostrand Rein-

hold, 1968), p. 5.

[15]Ibid., p. 4.

[16]Ibid., p. 83.

[17]See Abraham H. Maslow, *Religions, Values, and Peak Experiences* (New York: Viking, 1970); idem, *The Farther Reaches of Human Nature* (New York: Penguin, 1979).

[18]Maslow, *Farther Reaches,* p. 264.

[19]Goble, *Third Force,* pp. 15–16.

[20]Erich Fromm, *Escape from Freedom* (New York: Avon, 1967), p. 50.

[21]Erich Fromm, *Psychoanalysis and Religion* (New Haven: Yale University Press, 1971), p. 37.

[22]Ibid.

[23]D. T. Suzuki, Erich Fromm, Richard De Martino, *Zen Buddhism and Psychoanalysis* (New York: Harper and Row, 1970), p. 141.

[24]Alvin Toffler, *The Third Wave* (New York: Bantam, 1981), p. 366.

[25]Jeffrey Klein, "Esalen Slides off the Cliff," *Mother Jones,* December 1979, p. 26.

[26]Quoted in Charles T. Tart, ed., *Transpersonal Psychologies* (New York: Harper and Row, 1977), p. 2.

[27]Barry McWaters, *Conscious Evolution* (San Francisco: Institute for the Study of Conscious Evolution, 1981), p. 149.

[28]Wilber's use of "transpersonal" is not, strictly speaking, monistic but his overall world view is. See *No Boundary* (Boulder, Colo.: Shambhala, 1981); *Up from Eden* (Boulder, Colo.: Shambhala, 1983); and *A Sociable God* (New York: McGraw-Hill, 1983).

[29]See Klein, "Esalen Slides off the Cliff."

[30]Francis Adeney, "The Flowering of the Human Potential Movement," *Spiritual Counterfeits Journal* 5, no. 1 (Winter 1981), p. 13. I am indebted to this essay for much of the structure of my presentation.

[31]Ibid.

[32]Carl Raschke, "The Human Potential Movement," *Theology Today,* October 1976, p. 257.

[33]Ibid.

[34]Raschke, "Human Potential Movement," p. 258.

[35]Joel Latner, *The Gestalt Therapy Book* (New York: Julian Press, 1973), quoted in Raschke, "Human Potential Movement," p. 258.

[36]Leonard Geller, "The Failure of Self-Actualization Theory," *Journal of Humanistic Psychology* 22, no. 2 (Spring 1982), p. 60.

[37]Ibid., p. 61.

[38]Ibid., p. 63.

[39]Ibid., p. 64.

[40]Ibid.

[41]Maslow, *Toward a Psychology of Being,* p. 161.

[42]Geller, "Failure of Self-Actualization Theory," pp. 65–66.

[43]Paul Vitz, *Psychology as Religion* (Grand Rapids, Mich.: Eerdmans, 1977), p. 42.

[44]Ibid., pp. 42–44.

[45]David G. Myers, "The Inflated Self," *The Christian Century,* 1 December 1982, p. 1226.

[46]Ibid., pp. 1226–27

[47]Ibid., p. 1227.

⁴⁸Ibid.

⁴⁹Ibid.

⁵⁰Ibid.

⁵¹Ibid., p. 1228.

⁵²Ibid. See David G. Myers, _The Inflated Self_ (New York: Seabury Press, 1981), for more extensive documentation on the six streams.

⁵³See Myers, "Inflated Self," p. 1228.

⁵⁴Vitz, _Psychology as Religion_, pp. 46–47.

⁵⁵Blaise Pascal _Pensées_ 7.430.

⁵⁶G. K. Chesterton, _Orthodoxy_ (Garden City, N.Y.: Image Books, 1959), p. 21.

⁵⁷Pascal _Pensées_ 7.430.

⁵⁸Reinhold Niebhur, _The Nature and Destiny of Man_, 2 vols. (New York: Scribners, 1946), 1:16. See also Romans 1:18–32.

⁵⁹Augustine _City of God_ 14.13.

⁶⁰Myers, _Inflated Self_, pp. 41–42.

## Chapter Five: The New God of Science

¹Fred Alan Wolf, _Taking the Quantum Leap_ (San Francisco: Harper and Row, 1981), p. 63.

²Paul Davies, _Other Worlds_ (New York: Simon and Schuster, 1980), p. 75.

³Heinz R. Pagels, _The Cosmic Code: Quantum Physics as the Language of Nature_ (New York: Simon and Schuster, 1982), p. 89.

⁴Quoted in Paul Davies, _God and the New Physics_ (New York: Simon and Schuster, 1983), p. 100.

⁵Pagels, _Cosmic Code_, pp. 97–98.

⁶Capra, _Turning Point_, p. 80.

⁷Ibid., pp. 80–81.

⁸David Bohm, _Wholeness and the Implicate Order_ (London: Routledge and Kegan Paul, 1980).

⁹Ibid., p. 11.

¹⁰Capra, _Tao_, pp. 130–301.

¹¹Ferguson, _Aquarian_, p. 152.

¹²Capra, _Tao_, p. 140.

¹³Capra, _Turning Point_, p. 87.

¹⁴Wolf, _Quantum Leap_, p. 183.

¹⁵Leonard, _Silent Pulse_, p. 68.

¹⁶Ibid., p. 69.

¹⁷Ibid.

¹⁸Ibid., pp. 70ff.

¹⁹Quoted in Ferguson, _Aquarian_, p. 180.

²⁰Leonard, _Silent Pulse_, p. 73.

²¹Michael Talbot, _Mysticism and the New Physics_ (New York: Bantam, 1981), p. 14.

²²Ferguson, _Aquarian_, p. 182.

²³Jean Shinoda Bolen, _The Tao of Psychology: Synchronicity and the Self_ (New York: Harper and Row, 1979), p. 75.

²⁴"Update," _Brain-Mind Bulletin_, 16 April 1984, p. 3.

[25]For instance, see Martin Gardener, *Science: Good, Bad, and Bogus* (Buffalo, N.Y.: Prometheus, 1982).

[26]Russell Targ and Keith Haray, "An Inside View: Psi Research," *New Realities* 5, nos. 5-6, p. 78.

[27]Ronald M. McRae, "Psychic Warriors," *Omni*, April 1984, p. 60; and Ronald M. McRae, *Mind Wars* (New York: St. Martin's Press, 1984).

[28]See Kathleen Goss, "Psi in China: New Era of East West Cooperation," *New Realities* 5, nos. 5-6, pp. 46-51.

[29]Ian G. Barbour, *Issues in Science and Religion* (San Francisco: Harper Torchbooks, 1966), p. 287.

[30]Robert John Russell, "The Dancing Wu Li Masters: An Overview of the New Physics," a book review in *Zygon*, December 1980, p. 442.

[31]Gordon H. Clark, "The Limits and Use of Science," *Horizons of Science*, Carl Henry, ed. (New York: Harper and Row, 1978), p. 263.

[32]Gordon H. Clark, *A Christian View of Men and Things* (Grand Rapids, Mich.: Baker, 1981), p. 204.

[33]Ken Wilber, ed., *The Holographic Paradigm and Other Paradoxes* (Boulder, Colo.: Shambhala, 1982), p. 178.

[34]Ibid.

[35]Capra, *Turning Point*, p. 96.

[36]Capra, *Tao*, p. 11.

[37]Arthur F. Holmes, *Contours of a World View* (Grand Rapids, Mich.: Eerdmans, 1983), p. 44.

[38]Ibid., p. 41.

[39]Ibid.

[40]Anthony Standen, *Science Is a Sacred Cow* (New York: E. P. Dutton, 1950), p. 91.

[41]Ibid., p. 88.

[42]Stanley Jaki, *The Road of Science and the Ways to God* (Chicago: University of Chicago Press, 1980), p. 70.

[43]Paul Johnson, *Modern Times: The World from the Twenties to the Eighties* (New York: Harper and Row, 1983), pp. 1-4.

[44]Martin Gardener, *The Whys of a Philosophical Scrivener* (New York: Quill, 1983), pp. 87-88.

[45]Itzhak Bentov, *Stalking the Wild Pendulum: On the Mechanics of Consciousness* (New York: Bantam, 1979), p. 194.

[46]Talbot, *Mysticism*, p. 169.

[47]Richard H. Bube, "Science and Pseudo-Science," *The Reformed Journal*, November 1982, p. 11.

[48]Ibid., p. 13.

[49]Jaki, *Road of Science*, p. vii. This book gives a scholarly defense of this thesis.

[50]Abraham Kuyper, *The Work of the Holy Spirit* (1900; reprint ed., Grand Rapids, Mich.: Eerdmans, 1975), p. 44.

[51]Pascal *Pensées* 2.72.

[52]See Rousas John Rushdoony, *Institutes of Biblical Law* (Nutley, N.J.: Craig Press, 1973).

[53]See Christopher B. Kaiser, "Some Recent Developments in the Sciences and Their Relevance for Christian Theology," *Reformed Review* 29, no. 3 (Spring 1976), pp. 150-

52.

⁵⁴Capra, *Turning Point,* p. 29.

⁵⁵Myers, *The Inflated Self,* p. 93.

⁵⁶Sire, *Universe Next Door,* pp. 198–99.

⁵⁷Roszak, *Unfinished Animal,* p. 238.

⁵⁸I owe special thanks to Dean Halverson of Spiritual Counterfeits Project for his advice on this chapter.

**Chapter Six: The Politics of Transformation**

¹William Irwin Thompson, *Evil and World Order* (New York: Harper and Row, 1976), p. 15.

²Ferguson, *Aquarian,* p. 191.

³Rubin, *Growing Up,* p. 198.

⁴Ibid., p. 208.

⁵Mark Satin, *New Age Politics* (New York: Dell, 1979), pp. 269–85.

⁶Toffler, *Third Wave,* p. 9.

⁷Ibid.

⁸Ibid., p. 10.

⁹Satin, *New Age Politics,* pp. 7–51.

¹⁰Ibid., p. 7.

¹¹Capra, *Turning Point,* p. 46.

¹²Ibid., pp. 389–419. For a radically different and convincing perspective on natural resources and pollution see Julian Simon, *The Ultimate Resource* (Princeton, N.J.: Princeton University Press, 1981).

¹³Capra, *Turning Point,* p. 45.

¹⁴Charlene Spretnak, ed., *The Politics of Women's Spirituality* (Garden City, N.Y.: Anchor, 1982), p. xviii.

¹⁵Ibid., p. xvii.

¹⁶See, for instance, Satin's "New Age 'Political Platform,' " in Satin, *New Age Politics,* pp. 235–56, which advocates strong federal government and the political redistribution of wealth, despite some more politically conservative ideas such as decreasing the prominence of public education.

¹⁷Ibid., p. 149.

¹⁸Mumford, *Transformations,* p. 142.

¹⁹William Irwin Thompson, *Darkness and Scattered Light* (Garden City, N.Y.: Anchor, 1978), p. 13.

²⁰Satin, *New Age Politics,* pp. 149–52, 254.

²¹See Warren Wagnar, "Toward a World Set Free: The Vision of H. G. Wells," *The Futurist,* August 1983, pp. 25–31.

²²Donald Keys, *Earth at Omega: Passage to Planetization* (Boston: Branden Press, 1982), p. iii.

²³Ibid., p. 72.

²⁴Ibid., p. 43.

²⁵Ibid., p. 102.

²⁶*Initiator,* September 1983.

²⁷Ibid.

[28]For an outline of Alice Bailey's thought see *The Reappearance of the Christ* (New York: Lucis Trust, 1948).

[29]Benjamin Creme, *The Reappearance of the Christ and the Masters of Wisdom* (Los Angeles: Tara Press, 1980).

[30]Robert Muller, *New Genesis: Shaping a Global Spirituality* (Garden City, N.Y.: Doubleday, 1982), p. 49.

[31]Ferguson, *Aquarian*, p. 217.

[32]Ibid., p. 213.

[33]Ibid., pp. 62–63.

[34]Each congressperson elects whether to support the clearinghouse or not. If so, they give some of their staff budget to the clearinghouse. For more information write: Congressional Clearinghouse on the Future, Washington, D.C. 20515.

[35]" 'Transformation' Planks Become Part of Democratic Platform," *Leading Edge* 2, no. 14 (1982).

[36]"New 'Transformational' Ideas Enter Swedish Political Mainstream," *Renewal* 1, no. 2 (1981), p. 1.

[37]Fritjof Capra and Charlene Spretnak, "Who Are the Greens?" *New Age*, April 1984, p. 77. For a critique of the Green agenda see Allan C. Carlson, "The Green Alternative and the Deathwatch for Industrial Society," *Persuasion at Work*, September 1984, pp. 1–6.

[38]Ferguson, *Aquarian*, p. 236.

[39]Jim Channon, *Evolutionary Tactics* (privately printed, 1982). See also Ron McRae, *Mind Wars*, pp. 114–130.

[40]See Adeney, "Educators Look East," pp. 28–31.

[41]Lyn Smith, "Adult Type Education for School Children," *Los Angeles Times*, 24 June 1982.

[42]Quoted in Elliot Miller, "Saying No to the New Age," *Moody Monthly*, February 1985, p. 23.

[43]Satin, *New Age Politics*, pp. 250–51.

[44]Ferguson, *Aquarian*, p. 223.

[45]Keys, *Earth at Omega*, p. 88.

[46]Marie Jahoda, "Wholes and Parts, Meaning and Mechanism," *Nature* 296 (8 April 1982), p. 498.

[47]Satin, *New Age Politics*, p. 97; Rubin, *Growing Up*, p. 188.

[48]Ferguson, *Aquarian*, p. 381.

[49]Thompson, *From Nation to Emanation*, p. 84.

[50]David Spangler, *Reflections on the Christ* (Scotland: Findhorn, 1977), pp. 36–39.

[51]David Spangler, *Explorations: Emerging Aspects of the New Planetary Culture* (Scotland: Findhorn, 1980), p. 106.

[52]Doug Bandow, "The UN Goes for the Moon . . . Antarctica and the Ocean Floor," *Inquiry*, February 1984, p. 29.

[53]See Rousas J. Rushdoony, *The Politics of Guilt and Pity* (Fairfax, Va.: Thoburn Press, 1978), pp. 184–99 on the errors of the United Nations.

[54]G. K. Chesterton, *The Everlasting Man* (Garden City, N.Y.: Image Books, 1955), p. 246. See also Chesterton, *Orthodoxy*, pp. 133–34. For a Christian critique of statism see Herbert Schlossberg, *Idols for Destruction* (Nashville: Thomas Nelson, 1983), pp. 177–

231.

[55]Gary North, _The Dominion Covenant: Genesis_ (Tyler, Tex.: Institute for Christian Economics, 1982), p. 151.

## Chapter Seven: New Age Spirituality

[1]Harvey Cox, _Turning East_ (New York: Simon and Schuster, 1977), p. 139.

[2]Hunt, _Peace, Prosperity,_ p. 181.

[3]Cox, _Turning East,_ pp. 129–45.

[4]Rick Ingrasci, "Up from Eden: A New Age Interview with Ken Wilber," _New Age,_ April 1982, p. 77.

[5]See David G. Bromiley and Anson D. Shupe, _Strange Gods: The Great American Cult Scare_ (Boston: Beacon Press, 1981). While these authors give a needed perspective, they neglect the spiritual dynamic of cults. For a good overview of modern cults and their influence from a Christian viewpoint, see Enroth, _A Guide to Cults and New Religions._

[6]See Francis King, _Sexuality, Magic, and Perversion_ (Secaucus, N.J.: Citadel Press, 1971).

[7]Gordon Melton, "Witchcraft: An Inside View," _Christianity Today,_ 21 October 1983, p. 23. Unfortunately, Melton underestimates the dangers of witchcraft.

[8]Margot Adler, _Drawing Down the Moon: Witches, Druids, Goddess-Worshippers and Other Pagans in America Today_ (Boston: Beacon Press, 1979), p. v.

[9]See Mary Daly, _Beyond God the Father: Toward a Philosophy of Women's Liberation_ (Boston: Beacon Press, 1973).

[10]Adler, _Drawing Down the Moon,_ p. 149.

[11]Starhawk, _The Spiral Dance_ (San Francisco: Harper and Row, 1979), p. 9.

[12]See ibid. and Adler, _Drawing Down the Moon._

[13]Starhawk, _Spiral Dance,_ p. 129.

[14]Ibid., p. 135.

[15]Rosemary Ruether, "Goddesses and Witches: Liberation and Countercultural Feminism," _The Christian Century,_ 10 September 1980, p. 848.

[16]Ibid., p. 844; idem, _Sexism and God-Talk: Toward a Feminist Theology_ (Boston: Beacon Press, 1983), pp. 39–41, 47–52 for a general criticism of neo-pagan feminism.

[17]Adler, _Drawing Down the Moon,_ p. 187.

[18]Wilber, _Up from Eden,_ p. 70.

[19]Mark Mayell, "In Search of the Magic of Findhorn," _East/West Journal,_ January 1983, pp. 32–38.

[20]Adler, _Drawing Down the Moon,_ p. 197.

[21]Melton, "Witchcraft," p. 23.

[22]Theodore Roszak, _Person/Planet_ (Garden City, N.Y.: Anchor, 1978), p. 44.

[23]Carl F. H. Henry, _God, Revelation, and Authority,_ 6 vols. (Waco, Tex.: Word, 1976), 5:159.

[24]Susan Foh, _Women and the Word of God: A Response to Biblical Feminism_ (Grand Rapids, Mich.: Baker, 1980), pp. 144–63.

[25]Ibid., p. 153.

[26]C. S. Lewis, _God in the Dock_ (Grand Rapids, Mich.: Eerdmans, 1970), p. 237.

[27]Ruether, "Goddesses and Witches," p. 843.

28To understand the different strands of Hinduism, see R. C. Zaehner, *Hinduism* (New York: Oxford University Press, 1966).

29Swami Prabhavananda and Fredrick Manchester, *The Upanishads: Breath of the Eternal* (New York: Mentor, 1957), p. 70.

30Ibid., p. 73.

31Rajneesh, *I Am the Gate,* p. 17.

32Ibid., p. 15.

33Wilber, *Up from Eden,* p. 321.

34C. G. Jung, *Psychology and the East,* trans. R. F. C. Hull (Princeton, N.J.: Princeton University Press, 1978), pp. 174-75. On Christian meditation see Edmund Clowney, *Christian Meditation* (Nutley, N.J.: Craig Press, 1979); and Calvin Miller, *Transcendental Hesitation* (Grand Rapids, Mich.: Zondervan, 1977).

35Wilber, *A Sociable God,* p. 33.

36Rajneesh, *I Am the Gate,* p. 16.

37See especially the writings of Ken Wilber.

38Joseph Campbell, *The Masks of God: Occidental Mythology* (New York: Penguin, 1982), p. 3.

39Swami Prabhavananda and Christopher Isherwood, trans., *The Song of God: Bhagavad-Gita* (New York: Mentor, 1951), p. 36.

40Edward Rice, *Eastern Definitions* (New York: Anchor, 1980), pp. 398-99.

41Elaine Pagels, *The Gnostic Gospels* (New York: Vintage, 1981), p. 149.

42Robinson, *Nag Hammadi,* p. 126.

43Ibid., p. 129.

44MacLaine, *Out on a Limb,* p. 236.

45Christopher Hills, *The Christ Book: What Did He Really Say?* (Boulder Creek, Calif.: University of the Trees Press, 1980), p. 48.

46Levi, *The Aquarian Gospel of Jesus the Christ* (Marina Del Rey, Calif., 1981), p. 64.

47Ibid., p. 255.

48David Spangler, *Reflections on the Christ* (Scotland: Findhorn, 1978), p. 14.

49Ibid., p. 16.

50Wilber, *Up from Eden,* p. 134.

51Ibid., p. 244.

52James Sire, *Scripture Twisting: Twenty Ways Cults Misread the Bible* (Downers Grove, Ill.: InterVarsity Press, 1980).

53See John Warwick Montgomery, *History and Christianity* (Downers Grove, Ill.: InterVarsity Press, 1972); and F. F. Bruce, *The New Testament Documents: Are They Reliable?* (Downers Grove, Ill.: InterVarsity Press, 1960) for introductory material. On the apologetic use of Christian evidences see Thom Notaro, *Van Til and the Use of Evidence* (Phillipsburg, N.J.: Presbyterian and Reformed, 1980).

54Raymond Brown, book review of *The Gnostic Gospels, New York Times Book Review,* 20 January 1980, p. 3.

55Joseph Fitzmyer, "The Gospel According to Pagels," *America,* 16 February 1980, p. 123; see also Pheme Perkins, "Popularizing the Past," *Commonweal,* 9 November 1979, p. 535. See also Kathleen McVey, "Gnosticism, Feminism, and Elaine Pagels," *Theology Today,* January 1981, pp. 498-501.

56See Hunt, *Peace, Prosperity,* p. 102.

⁵⁷For a summary of Christ's fulfillment of prophecy see Josh McDowell, *Evidence That Demands a Verdict* (Arrowhead Springs, Calif.: Campus Crusade for Christ, 1973), pp. 147–84.

⁵⁸Cited in Mark Albrecht, *Reincarnation: A Christian Appraisal* (Downers Grove, Ill.: InterVarsity Press, 1982), p. 9.

⁵⁹Quoted in ibid., p. 21.

⁶⁰"False 'Memories' May Reduce Legal Value of Hypnosis," *Brain-Mind Bulletin* 9 (12 December 1983), p. 1. See also Elizabeth Stark, "Hypnosis on Trial," *Psychology Today,* February 1984, pp. 34–36.

⁶¹For a detailed argument against reincarnation from a Christian viewpoint, see Albrecht, *Reincarnation.*

⁶²John R. W. Stott, *Basic Christianity* (Downers Grove, Ill.: InterVarsity Press, 1971), p. 27.

⁶³R. C. Zaehner, *Our Savage God: The Perverse Use of Eastern Thought* (New York: Sheed and Ward, 1974), p. 71.

⁶⁴Ibid., p. 72.

⁶⁵Ibid., p. 69.

⁶⁶Vincent Bugliosi, *Helter Skelter* (New York: Bantam, 1975), p. 300.

⁶⁷Ibid., p. 317.

⁶⁸Ibid., p. 637; Manson also believed in a master race and referred to Hitler as "a tuned-in guy who had leveled the karma of the Jews," p. 317.

⁶⁹Nigel Davies, *Human Sacrifice in History and Today* (New York: William Morrow, 1981), p. 86.

⁷⁰Ibid., p. 95.

⁷¹Ibid., p. 96.

⁷²Ananda K. Coomarswamy, *Hinduism and Buddhism* (New York: The Philosophical Library, n.d.), p. 30.

⁷³See Keith Yandell, "On Windowless Experiences," *Christian Scholars Review* 4, no. 4 (1975), pp. 311–18.

⁷⁴Henry, *God, Revelation and Authority,* 1:70.

⁷⁵Paul Weiss, *The God We Seek* (Carbondale, Ill.: Southern Illinois University Press, 1973), p. 150.

⁷⁶W. C. Irvine, ed., *Heresies Exposed* (Neptune, N.J.: Loizeaux Brothers, 1921), p. 98.

⁷⁷Quoted in Donald Bloesch, *Faith and Its Counterfeits* (Downers Grove, Ill.: InterVarsity Press, 1981), p. 74. On the lostness of the heathen, see J. Oswald Sanders, *How Lost Are the Heathen?* (Chicago, Ill: Moody Press, 1972).

**Chapter Eight: Challenging the One for All**

¹From promotional materials.

²Quoted in Robert Tucker, "Back to Basics: The New Age Conspiracy," *New Age Source,* February 1983, p. 10. See also Norman Boucher, "Transforming the Corporation," *New Age Journal,* February 1985, pp. 36–44. For the testimony of an ex–New Age business seminar speaker see *Testimony of a New Ager: An Interview with Mr. Ed Steele and Joseph Todd* (Oklahoma City, Okla.: Southwest Radio Church, 1983). This can be ordered from Southwest Radio Church, P.O. Box 1144, Oklahoma City, OK 73101.

[3]Gary North, *None Dare Call It Witchcraft* (New Rochelle, N.Y.: Arlington House, 1976), p. 185.

[4]Ferguson, *Aquarian,* pp. 210-12.

[5]See Rousas John Rushdoony, "Power from Below," *The Journal of Christian Reconstruction* 1, no. 2 (Winter 1974), pp. 7-10.

[6]See Myers, *Inflated Self,* pp. 43-119.

[7]Chesterton, *Orthodoxy,* p. 54.

[8]Charles Fair, *The New Nonsense* (New York: Simon and Schuster, 1974), p. 27; see also Christopher Evans, *Cults of Unreason* (New York: Delta, 1973); and, from a Christian perspective, Danny Korem and Paul Meier, *The Fakers* (Grand Rapids, Mich.: Baker, 1980).

[9]Gordon Ratray Taylor, *The Natural History of the Mind* (New York: Penguin, 1979), p. 111.

[10]Martin Buber, *Between Man and Man* (New York: Macmillan, 1965), p. 24.

[11]Ibid.

[12]Ibid.

[13]North, *The Dominion Covenant,* pp. 1-11.

[14]Chesterton, *Orthodoxy,* p. 131.

[15]Donald G. Bloesch, *Essentials of Evangelical Theology,* 2 vols. (New York: Harper and Row, 1979), 1:34.

[16]See Stephen G. Meyer, "Neuropsychology and Worship," *Journal of Psychology and Theology* 3, no. 4 (Fall 1975), pp. 281-89.

[17]Meister Eckhart is a prime example. On Eckhart see Thomas Molnar, *God and the Knowledge of Reality* (New York: Basic Books, 1973), pp. 38-41. For a survey of the Christian mystical tradition, both orthodox and unorthodox, see Evelyn Underhill, *Mysticism* (New York: E. P. Dutton, 1961).

[18]Kuyper, *Work of the Holy Spirit,* p. 333.

[19]See R. J. Rushdoony, *By What Standard?* (Fairfax, Va.: Thoburn Press, 1958), pp. 96-97.

[20]Much of modern positive thinking can be traced to the pantheistic New Thought movement of mid-nineteenth century America. See Dean Halverson, "Mind Power: A History and Analysis of the New Thought Movement," *Spiritual Counterfeits Newsletter* 11, no. 1 (Spring 1985), pp. 1ff.; and Carl A. Raschke, *The Interruption of Eternity* (Chicago: Nelson-Hall, 1980), pp. 174-201. For a critique of positive thinking, positive confession, and visualization in the church see Dave Hunt and T. A. McMahon, *The Seduction of Christianity* (Eugene, Oreg.: Harvest House, 1985).

[21]John Calvin *Institutes of the Christian Religion* 2.2.15.

[22]See Elliot Miller, "Saying No to the New Age," pp. 22-25.

[23]For a discussion of how pantheism adversely affects cultures see North, *None Dare Call It Witchcraft,* pp. 171-81.

# Related Reading

This brief listing does not attempt to be comprehensive. None of the following books are written from the New Age perspective (with the possible exception of *Mind Wars*), and most are written from a Christian perspective. These books will often be more helpful for Christians than the New Age books themselves.

## General Critiques of the New Age

Constance Cumbey. *Hidden Dangers of the Rainbow.* Shreveport, La.: Huntington House, 1983. Contains much pertinent information on the New Age, but I think it suffers from, first, an overemphasis on the role Alice Bailey's teachings play in the New Age; second, an implausible application of biblical prophesy to the New Age; third, sometimes uncritical accusations against Christians purported to be involved in the New Age; fourth, an unlikely conspiracy theory; fifth, an unlikely equation of the New Age with Nazism; and sixth, somewhat spotty documentation.

"Empowering the Self: A Look at the Human Potential Movement." *Spiritual Counterfeits Project Journal.* Winter 1981-82. Excellent.

Os Guinness. *The Dust of Death.* Downers Grove, Ill.: InterVarsity Press, 1973. Classic Christian assessment of the counterculture. It is helpful for understanding the roots of the New Age movement.

Dave Hunt. *The Cult Explosion.* Irvine, Calif.: Harvest House, 1980.

Dave Hunt. *Peace, Prosperity, and the Coming Holocaust.* Eugene, Oreg.: Harvest House, 1983. Mr. Hunt is a good researcher and is on top of the New Age movement. Even those who don't agree with his end-time emphasis and connection of the New Age movement with Nazism will benefit from his work.

Gary North. *None Dare Call It Witchcraft.* New Rochelle, N.Y.: Arlington House, 1976. Thorough analysis of occult and countercultural themes. Best overall critique written before the term *New Age* caught on.

James Sire. *Scripture Twisting.* Downers Grove, Ill.: InterVarsity Press, 1980. Shows twenty ways cults misinterpret the Bible for their own ends. Good for understanding how the New Age movement distorts the Bible.

James Sire. *The Universe Next Door.* Downers Grove, Ill.: InterVarsity Press, 1976. Excellent chapters on "Eastern Pantheistic Monism" and "The New Consciousness" from a world-view perspective.

Clifford Willson and John Weldon. *Occult Shock and Psychic Forces.* San Diego, Calif.:

Master Books, 1980. Encyclopedic treatment of many aspects of occult/New Age thinking from a Christian viewpoint.

## Holistic Health

Martin Bobgan and Diedre Bobgan. *Hypnosis and the Christian.* Minneapolis, Minn.: Bethany House, 1984. Short but provocative critique of hypnosis.

Paul C. Reisser, Teri K. Reisser and John Weldon. *The Holistic Healers.* Downers Grove, Ill.: InterVarsity Press, 1983. Excellent Christian critique.

*Spiritual Counterfeits Journal.* August 1978. Focuses on holistic health and contains several important articles.

John Weldon and Zola Levitt. *Psychic Healing.* Chicago, Ill.: Moody Press, 1982. In-depth Christian treatment of the occult side of holistic health.

## New Age Science, Parapsychology

Mark Albrecht and Brooks Alexander. "The Sellout of Science." *Spiritual Counterfeits Journal.* August 1978, pp. 19-29. A pioneering critique of New Age physics from a Christian world view.

"Expanding Horizons: Psychical Research and Parapsychology." *Spiritual Counterfeits Journal.* Winter 1980. Excellent issue full of helpful articles.

Ron MacRae. *Mind Wars.* New York: St. Martin's Press, 1985. A journalist's appraisal of United States military interest in parapsychology ("psychic weapons").

## Psychology

Martin Bobgan and Deidre Bobgan. *The Psychological Way/The Spiritual Way.* Minneapolis, Minn.: Bethany Fellowship, 1979. Analysis of major psychological schools including New Age practices.

William Kirk Kilpatrick. *Psychological Seduction.* Nashville, Tenn.: Nelson, 1983. A strong antidote to New Age and secular selfism, plus many positive Christian insights.

David Myers. *The Inflated Self.* New York: Seabury Press, 1980. Insights into modern psychology's findings concerning human selfishness and illusions. Evidence against New Age view of innate human goodness.

Paul Vitz. *Psychology as Religion.* Grand Rapids, Mich.: Eerdmans, 1977. Exposes modern psychology as a new religion. Critiques influential psychologists such as Maslow and Rogers.

## Spirituality, Cults, Comparative Religion

Mark Albrecht. *Reincarnation: A Christian Appraisal.* Downers Grove, Ill.: InterVarsity Press, 1982. Thorough assessment and refutation of reincarnation. Excellent.

Norman Anderson. *Christianity and World Religions.* Downers Grove, Ill.: InterVarsity Press, 1984. Evangelical study of the uniqueness of Christianity and its relationship to other religions.

Ronald Enroth and others. *A Guide to Cults and New Religions.* Downers Grove, Ill.: InterVarsity Press, 1983. Essays on traditional and New Age religious movements from a Christian perspective.

Richard Grenier. *The Gandhi Nobody Knows.* Nashville, Tenn.: Nelson, 1983. Gandhi is much revered by the New Age, but much of his life is ignored. Grenier also emphasizes the devastating effect Hinduism has had on India.

Dave Hunt and T. A. McMahon. *The Seduction of Christianity.* Eugene, Oreg.: Harvest House, 1985. Well-documented study of how unbiblical New Age ideas are infiltrating the church. Sometimes too heavy-handed.

Carl A. Raschke. *The Interruption of Eternity: Modern Gnosticism and the Origins of the New Religious Consciousness.* Chicago, Ill.: Nelson-Hall, 1980. Scholarly study of the background and emergence of the New Age viewpoint. Excellent.

## Politics

Ed Rowe. *New Age Globalism.* Herndon, Va.: Growth Publishing, 1985. Short overview of New Age and humanistic political goals. Doesn't adequately distinguish secular humanism from the New Age movement.

Herbert Schlossberg. *Idols for Destruction.* Nashville, Tenn.: Nelson, 1983. Although not directly related to the New Age movement, Schlossberg's superb political analysis touches on many aspects of New Age politics.

## Testimonies

Rabi Maharaj. *Escape into the Light.* Eugene, Oreg.: Harvest House, 1984. An Indian guru turns to Christ.

Caryl Matrisciana. *Gods of the New Age.* Eugene, Oreg.: Harvest House, 1985. Some points are inadequately documented. Interesting material on the miseries of Hinduism in India.

Elissa Lindsey McClain. *Rest from the Quest.* Shreveport, La.: Huntington House, 1984. A long-time devotee comes to Christ.

## Organizations

Christian Research Institute. P.O. Box 500, San Juan Capistrano, CA 92693-0500. Publishes a quarterly journal, *Forward,* which covers cults and issues related to the New Age.

Jesus People USA. 4707 N. Malden, Chicago, IL 60640. Provides tracts on the New Age and publishes the magazine *Cornerstone.*

Spiritual Counterfeits Project. P.O. Box 4308, Berkeley, CA 94704. Publishes an informative newsletter and a journal. SCP has done some of the best work on cults and New Age issues.

# Index